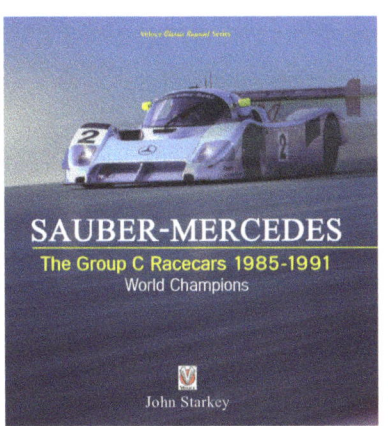

More books from Veloce...

- 1½-litre GP Racing 1961-1965 (Whitelock)
- AC Two-litre Saloons & Buckland Sportscars (Archibald)
- Alfa Romeo 155/156/147 Competition Touring Cars (Collins)
- Alfa Tipo 33 (McDonough & Collins)
- Alpine & Renault – The Development of the Revolutionary Turbo F1 Car 1968 to 1979 (Smith)
- Autodrome (Collins & Ireland)
- Bahamas Speed Weeks, The (O'Neil)
- British at Indianapolis, The (Wagstaff)
- British Café Racers (Cloesen)
- Bugatti Type 40 (Price)
- Bugatti 46/50 Updated Edition (Price & Arbey)
- Bugatti T44 & T49 (Price & Arbey)
- Bugatti 57 2nd Edition (Price)
- Bugatti Type 57 Grand Prix – A Celebration (Tomlinson)
- Cosworth – The Search for Power (6th edition) (Robson)
- Daily Mirror 1970 World Cup Rally 40, The (Robson)
- Datsun Fairlady Roadster to 280ZX – The Z-Car Story (Long)
- Fate of the Sleeping Beauties, The (op de Weegh/ Hottendorff/op de Weegh)
- Ferrari 288 GTO, The Book of the (Sackey)
- Ferrari 333 SP (O'Neil)
- Formula One – The Real Score? (Harvey)
- Formula 5000 Motor Racing, Back then ... and back now (Lawson)
- Forza Minardi! (Vigar)
- Grand Prix Ferrari – The Years of Enzo Ferrari's Power, 1948-1980 (Pritchard)
- Grand Prix Ford – DFV-powered Formula 1 Cars (Robson)
- GT – The World's Best GT Cars 1953-73 (Dawson)
- Italian Cafe Racers (Cloesen)
- Jaguar E-type Factory and Private Competition Cars (Griffiths)
- Lamborghini Miura Bible, The (Sackey)
- Lamborghini Murciélago, The book of the (Pathmanathan)
- Lamborghini Urraco, The Book of the (Landsem)
- Lancia 037 (Collins)
- Le Mans Panoramic (Ireland)
- Lexus Story, The (Long)
- Lola – The Illustrated History (1957-1977) (Starkey)
- Lola – All the Sports Racing & Single-seater Racing Cars 1978-1997 (Starkey)
- Lola T70 – The Racing History & Individual Chassis Record – 4th Edition (Starkey)
- Lotus 18 Colin Chapman's U-turn (Whitelock)
- Lotus 49 (Oliver)
- Making a Morgan (Hensing)
- Maserati 250F In Focus (Pritchard)
- Mazda MX-5/Miata 1.6 Enthusiast's Workshop Manual (Grainger & Shoemark)
- Mazda MX-5/Miata 1.8 Enthusiast's Workshop Manual (Grainger & Shoemark)
- Mazda MX-5 Miata, The book of the – The 'Mk1' NA-series 1988 to 1997 (Long)
- Mazda MX-5 Miata, The book of the – The 'Mk2' NB-series 1997 to 2004 (Long)
- Mazda MX-5 Miata Roadster (Long)
- Mazda Rotary-engined Cars (Cranswick)
- Mercedes-Benz SL – R230 series 2001 to 2011 (Long)
- Mercedes-Benz SL – W113-series 1963-1971 (Long)
- Mercedes-Benz SL & SLC – 107-series 1971-1989 (Long)
- Mercedes-Benz SLK – R170 series 1996-2004 (Long)
- Mercedes-Benz SLK – R171 series 2004-2011 (Long)
- Mercedes-Benz W123-series – All models 1976 to 1986 (Long)
- MG, Made in Abingdon (Frampton)
- MGB – The Illustrated History, Updated Fourth Edition (Wood & Burrell)
- Mike the Bike – Again (Macauley)
- Mitsubishi Lancer Evo, The Road Car & WRC Story (Long)
- Montlhéry, The Story of the Paris Autodrome (Boddy)
- Morris Minor, 70 Years on the Road (Newell)
- Moto Guzzi Sport & Le Mans Bible, The (Falloon)
- The Moto Guzzi Story – 3rd Edition (Falloon)
- Motor Racing – Reflections of a Lost Era (Carter)
- Motor Racing – The Pursuit of Victory 1930-1962 (Carter)
- Motor Racing – The Pursuit of Victory 1963-1972 (Wyatt/Sears)
- Motor Racing Heroes – The Stories of 100 Greats (Newman)
- Motorcycle GP Racing in the 1960s (Pereira)
- Motorsport In colour, 1950s (Wainwright)
- N.A.R.T. – A concise history of the North American Racing Team 1957 to 1983 (O'Neil)
- Nissan 300ZX & 350Z – The Z-Car Story (Long)
- Nissan GT-R Supercar: Born to race (Gorodji)
- Northeast American Sports Car Races 1950-1959 (O'Neil)
- Porsche 911R, RS & RSR, 4th Edition (Starkey)
- Porsche 930 to 935: The Turbo Porsches (Starkey)
- Racing Colours – Motor Racing Compositions 1908-2009 (Newman)
- Racing Line – British motorcycle racing in the golden age of the big single (Guntrip)
- Rallye Sport Fords: The Inside Story (Moreton)
- Rootes Cars of the 50s, 60s & 70s – Hillman, Humber, Singer, Sunbeam & Talbot, A Pictorial History (Rowe)
- Rover Cars 1945 to 2005, A Pictorial History
- Rover P4 (Bobbitt)
- Runways & Racers (O'Neil)
- RX-7 – Mazda's Rotary Engine Sportscar (Updated & Revised New Edition) (Long)
- Schlumpf – The intrigue behind the most beautiful car collection in the world (Op de Weegh & Op de Weegh)
- Sleeping Beauties USA – abandoned classic cars & trucks (Marek)
- Speedway – Auto racing's ghost tracks (Collins & Ireland)
- Subaru Impreza: The Road Car And WRC Story (Long)
- This Day in Automotive History (Corey)
- TT Talking – The TT's most exciting era – As seen by Manx Radio TT's lead commentator 2004-2012 (Lambert)
- Two Summers – The Mercedes-Benz W196R Racing Car (Ackerson)
- TWR Story, The – Group A (Hughes & Scott)
- Unraced (Collins)
- You & Your Jaguar XK8/XKR – Buying, Enjoying, Maintaining, Modifying – New Edition (Thorley)
- Wolseley Cars 1948 to 1975 (Rowe)
- Works Rally Mechanic (Moylan)

Veloce's other imprints:

www.veloce.co.uk

First published in 2002 by Gryfon Press. Veloce Classic Reprint (hardback) edition published December 2018. This (paperback) edition published March 2019 by Veloce Publishing Limited, Veloce House, Parkway Farm Business Park, Middle Farm Way, Poundbury, Dorchester DT1 3AR, England. Tel +44 (0)1305 260068 / Fax 01305 250479 / e-mail info@veloce.co.uk / web www.veloce.co.uk or www.velocebooks.com. ISBN: 978-1-787114-93-7 UPC: 6-36847-01493-3

© 2019 John Starkey and Veloce Publishing. All rights reserved. With the exception of quoting brief passages for the purpose of review, no part of this publication may be recorded, reproduced or transmitted by any means, including photocopying, without the written permission of Veloce Publishing Ltd. Throughout this book logos, model names and designations, etc, have been used for the purposes of identification, illustration and decoration. Such names are the property of the trademark holder as this is not an official publication. Readers with ideas for automotive books, or books on other transport or related hobby subjects, are invited to write to the editorial director of Veloce Publishing at the above address. British Library Cataloguing in Publication Data – A catalogue record for this book is available from the British Library. Typesetting, design and page make-up all by Veloce Publishing Ltd on Apple Mac. Printed and bound by CPI Group (UK) Ltd, Croydon, CR0 4YY.

Veloce Classic Reprint Series

SAUBER-MERCEDES
The Group C Racecars 1985-1991
World Champions

John Starkey

ACKNOWLEDGEMENTS

Writing a book on international motor racing is always an honor, as the author gets to talk with people who are masters of the fastest cars in the world. Not only that, most of these people are totally dedicated to their craft, whether as a driver, team manager, engineer or mechanic.

I am indebted first of all to Jochen Mass who, with his background as an F1 driver and his vast experience in all the greatest Sports and GT cars of his period, proved a veritable font of wisdom on the Sauber-Mercedes cars and team.

Leo Ress, Sauber's designer, was interviewed whilst in the middle of designing next year's Sauber F1 car. Nevertheless, he took the time and trouble to answer my questions when time must have been pressing. Thank you for your patience, Mr. Ress.

One of the world's best team managers and engineers, Dave Price, proved to be a wealth of information. Incidentally, it was Dave Price's Company, DPI Composites, who built the C11 and C291 chassis in England.

Kenny Acheson, who drove for the team in 1988, remembered his days of driving – *"The best of the bunch, really"* – with great fondness. Bob Bell, who went to Mercedes with Dave Price, also gave freely of his time whilst reminiscing about the great cars that he had engineered.

I should also like to thank both the Daimler-Chrysler archives and LAT Photographs of England for some really wonderful photographs for use in the book, and also to Daniel Mainzer, who took the photographs of Jochen Mass.

Michael Lauer, who races the ex-Schumacher C11 today was the inspiration behind this book, as he so loves his Mercedes racecar. Thank you, Michael.

Finally, to Su, our designer, who spent endless hours at the computer, cajoling me to "dot the i's and cross the t's." Thanks, Su; you did a great job.

JOHN STARKEY

DEDICATION

TO PETER SAUBER

TABLE OF CONTENTS

Introduction	....	vii
Chapter One	Beginnings	1
Chapter Two	Mercedes Engine Development	11
Chapter Three	Mercedes in 1988	15
Chapter Four	Mercedes Engine Development 1988-1989	29
Chapter Five	Sauber-Mercedes in 1989	37
Chapter Six	Mercedes Developments 1989-1990	63
Chapter Seven	Mercedes Racing in 1990	71
Chapter Eight	Fresh Start – The C291	87
Chapter Nine	1991 – The Final Season	91
Appendix	Individual Cars' Histories	105

FOREWORD

I have been a very lucky man, having had a long career in both F1 and sports cars. During my time at the wheel, I've driven a large number of cars, including the turbocharged Porsche 935, 936, 956 and 962, the 1974 Cosworth, Ford Mirage and Alfa T33.

In my opinion, not many cars deserve the title "great" when looking back at them. However, one make that does is certainly the Mercedes and Sauber-Mercedes C series of cars that I was fortunate to drive from 1988 to 1991.

The first cars that I drove, the C9's, were fast and responsive and well able to deal with the opposition from Porsche and TWR Jaguar. I had driven the 962C and can vouch that the Sauber-Mercedes C9 was a much superior car in every way.

When it came to the C11, that was an advance over the C9 and 1989 was a tremendous year for us all on the team. My co-driver Jean-Louis Schlesser took the Drivers' World Championship by the end of the year whilst I, along with Manuel Reuter and Stanley Dickens, won Le Mans, for me a long-standing goal.

The C291 of 1990 was a completely new car, of course. This time, we were racing a 3.5-liter normally aspirated car instead of the V8 5-liter turbocharged car. But yet again, Leo Ress had succeeded in producing a magical car. Fast, light and nimble, after some teething problems, the C291 proved yet again to be a winner just before Mercedes bowed out of racing at the end of 1991.

In 1990 and 1991, I had the pleasure of tutoring the three youngsters who were brought into the team to learn to drive "big" cars. The way that Karl Wendlinger, Heinz-Harald Frentzen and, of course, Michael Schumacher took to the 800 horsepower Mercedes was a revelation and a very pleasurable period for me.

If you are a fan of big, powerful, good-looking Sports-Prototypes, I believe there are none finer than these great Sauber designed, Mercedes engined cars. Through my association with Michael Lauer, I am still able to race these cars in vintage events in the USA. It is always a pleasure to drive onto the track in that wonderful car, the Sauber-Mercedes C11.

JOCHEN MASS
Monaco
October 2002

INTRODUCTION

A great era of racing took place in the eighties and early nineties. Blindingly fast Group C and GTP cars were created to run on either side of the Atlantic and the Pacific. They battled it out across America, Europe and Japan.

In Europe, these latter day Sports-prototypes, with their genesis being the Porsche 917's, Ferrari 512's and Lola T70's of the late 1960's, gained ground effects, turbocharging and, later on, electronically controlled engine management systems to make the most of every last drop of fuel allocated.

This latter innovation was important for cars needing to make pitstops and take on fuel. It was especially important for the Group C prototypes of Europe and Japan, where a fuel allocation formula was in force, making a necessity of frugality, combined with speed.

Of course, Mercedes have been arguably the most successful racing car constructor of all time, venturing out to race when they chose, securing Championships and then, having learned all they needed to know, withdrawing to use the experience gained to further their road car designs.

If you look at a Sauber-Mercedes Group C car from this period, it becomes obvious that money was no object in Mercedes' desire to win Championships. That can only be said about one other competitor from this period: Nissan. Of course, the Nissans never succeeded against the Sauber-Mercedes team but the story may have been different had Mercedes taken on the Electramotive and NPTI Nissans in America. They didn't and we shall never know who might have emerged the victor now.

These were, and are, great cars. Very powerful, with over 1000 horsepower on occasions, very fast, endowed with the greatest downforce of any of these cars and with an aura about them that reeked of serious intent.

JOHN STARKEY
September 2002

ABOUT THE AUTHOR

John Starkey is a self-confessed racing fanatic, having written many books on the subject, including; *Ferrari 250 GT Tour de France, Lola T70, The Racing History, The Racing Porsches, R to RSR*, with Ken Wells – *Lola, The Illustrated History (Parts I & II), Ferrari – Fifty Years on the Track, Ferrari 166 to F50 GT – The Racing Berlinettas, 930 to 935 – The Turbo Porsches, Racing with a Difference – The History of IMSA, Corvette – Fifty Years of Rolling Thunder, Lightning Speed – The Nissan GTP & Group C Racecars,* and *A Long & Deadly Season (a Novel).*

John has owned and raced two Ferraris, a 'Tour de France' Berlinetta and a Drogo-bodied 250GT Berlinetta, a Lola T70, a Porsche 935, and an ex–IMSA March 84G. He has campaigned a Lola T70 (his 3rd) in HSR events. Most of John's spare time is spent building and flying model airplanes – racers, of course.

John Starkey pictured with his Drogo-bodied Ferrari 250GT Berlinetta. [Courtesy of Bernard Starkey.]

Front Cover:
Mercedes C11 'Into dusk' – digital artwork by: Jeff 'Jai' Danton, of Veloce Publishing

Peter Sauber photograph page 3:
[Courtesy of Daimler-Chrysler Archives.]

CHAPTER 1

Photo: Courtesy of LAT

Beginnings

Sauber-Mercedes

The origins of the Group C Mercedes that reached fruition and success in the late 1980s and early 1990s, lie in Switzerland, instead of Stuttgart, where Mercedes' headquarters and factory are located. There, in Hinwil near Zurich, Peter Sauber began building his own two-liter Sports-racing cars in 1970. The C1-C4 series of Group 6 cars started with Volkswagen four-cylinder engines and ended with Cosworth units.

The C5 was powered by the BMW M12 two-liter four-cylinder engine. Sauber's first car to be entered at Le Mans was a special version of this car, fitted with a BMW M1 six-cylinder engine. This had a tube-frame chassis and the bodywork was in carbon-fiber, built by Seger and Hoffman Aerospace.

Dieter Quester bought the little coupe and, together with Marc Surer and David Deacon, Quester entered the car as a "BMW M1" for the Le Mans 24-Hour race in 1981. After 207 laps, the car retired with engine failure. At the Nürburgring 1000 kms race later that year, a second car won outright giving a tremendous fillip to the little Company. The drivers were Hans Stuck and Nelson Piquet.

Peter Sauber followed up his C5 with the SHS (Sieger and Hoffman Aerospace) C6 Group C car that he designed himself. Sieger and Hoffman built the aluminum monocoque chassis and carbon-fiber bodywork and Walter Brun, the slot machine racing millionaire, bought the car. Heini Mader supplied the 3.9-liter Cosworth DFL engines.

Two cars were entered for 1982, one to be driven by Siggi Muller and Walter Brun and to be maintained and run by Peter Sauber's own team, and one other car was sold to Gerhard Schneider's GS tuning company for Hans Stuck and Hans Heyer to drive. Ford Switzerland provided sponsorship for the "works" car.

Sadly, the 3.9 DFL Cosworth had a major vibration problem that mitigated against any significant results in 1982. At Le Mans, both cars, with spectacular red and white striped bodywork, retired with problems associated with this engine vibration. Later on in the year, Schneider had TC Prototypes in England modify their car to take an engine mounting subframe, to help lessen the vibration problem whilst Brun's car switched to BMW 1.7-liter turbocharged engines. Brun later on bought the GS car when that team encountered financial trouble.

At Mugello, the Brun/Muller duo drove their car to 5th place and Stuck shone at Brands Hatch in typically English rainy conditions. Walter Brun then took over the two cars and called them "Sehcars".

The Group C Racecars – World Champions

Peter Sauber. A racer with vision, Peter Sauber started his own Company to produce Group 6 two-liter Sports-racing cars and today runs his own Formula One team, using Ferrari built engines. [Photo: Courtesy of LAT.]

Roland Bassaleur bought one of the BMW M1-engined C6s and campaigned it at Le Mans and elsewhere for many years. Today, the car resides in America, where it is frequently raced in GTP events. [Photo: Authors collection.]

Peter Sauber then drew up the C7, learning from the C6 and making the car capable of handling a variety of engine installations. Rudi Faul designed the bodywork and just one BMW M1-powered example was built.

At Le Mans in 1983, the Sauber, driven by the IMSA team of Tony Garcia, Albert Naon and Diego Montoya, ran well to finish ninth, this car alone stopping Porsche from sweeping the top ten positions outright with their 956. Porsche issued a poster with the headline "No-one is perfect!" to commemorate the occasion. The car did a few other races, usually succeeding in placing in the top ten but, by now, Peter Sauber was back at the drawing board, designing the C76, which was intended to use a 3.5-liter engine.

For the bodywork of this car, Peter Sauber approached the Mercedes factory in Stuttgart for permission to use their wind tunnel. The Mercedes Company gave Sauber not only the nod (thus initiating a partnership that was to bring success, though not immediately, to both companies) but also suggested to Peter Sauber that he might like to use the new Mercedes M117 5-liter V8 engine. Thus resulted the Sauber-Mercedes C8.

Once again, the C8 was an aluminum monocoque chassis with new Peter Faul-designed bodywork of Kevlar-reinforced glass-fiber. The major change from the previous cars was, however, in the engine bay. There nestled the Mercedes production-based 5-liter V8, mildly blown through twin KKK turbochargers. This Heini Mader-developed engine produced some 700-plus

The Sauber C8 with Mercedes V8 power of 1986. This is the car driven by Henri Pescarolo and John Nielsen at Monza, where it finished ninth overall in the 1000 kms race of that year. [Photo: Courtesy of LAT.]

horsepower and made the new Sauber C8-Mercedes competitive right out of the box. The dry-sump two valve per cylinder V8 featured a linerless aluminum block with twin KKK turbochargers, one each per bank of four cylinders, fitted on each side. Air to air intercoolers were fitted and the engine management system was the Bosch Motronic 1.2 unit, similar to that employed on the Porsche 962. Maximum boost was 1.0 bar with .08 bar used in races. Maximum power was developed at a comparatively low 6,600 rpm. Of course, torque was tremendous from such a large, comparatively understressed engine.

In 1985, the car appeared first of all at Le Mans, where the C8, driven at the time by John Nielsen, took off and completed almost an entire loop before landing back on its wheels during practice. Although repairable, the car was not run in the race itself. It was later discovered that the "flight" had been caused by the undertray coming loose.

Leo Ress had worked on suspension design at both Mercedes and BMW. Leo Ress remembered: "I had first met Peter Sauber in 1981 and, in 1985, I moved, at his request, to Hinwil, to work on designing what became the C9. We designed this, using a wind tunnel, although this was one with a static floor. The aerodynamics were quite good. Prior to the C9, the Saubers that had gone before had no real aerodynamics."

"Obviously, our car was superior to the then dominant Porsche 962, as I think the designers had problems with that car, because the flat-six engine of the 962 did not allow the best of underbody aerodynamics." Leo Ress later recounted to the author that, when he joined the Sauber Company in 1985, there were just six full-time employees there!

For 1986, sponsorship was obtained from Kouros, the cosmetics producers, and Mike Thackwell and Henri Pescarolo were the nominated drivers. Despite their high level of professionalism, the Sauber team was still mainly a part-time operation, even Max Welti, Sauber's team manager, was not fully employed.

Although not being (quite!) able to catch the Porsche 962s and the TWR Jaguars, the Sauber-Mercedes was a good reliable package and in the rain-hit Nürburgring 1000 kms, Mike Thackwell and Henri Pescarolo lapped the field twice to take the win.

Things looked encouraging for 1987 and the car evolved into the Leo Ress-designed C9, now with the monocoque reinforced with bonded aluminum panels, improved ground effects and a front-mounted water radiator. At the rear, the suspension featured the coil spring/damper units mounted horizontally along the top engine support cradle tubes and operated through rockers. Wheels were now seventeen inches diameter (fronts) and nineteen inches diameter at the rear. Previously, the C8 had featured sixteen inch diameter wheels all around. Tire supplies

1986 Kouros 1000 kms race at Silverstone. Mike Thackwell, John Nielsen and Henri Pescarolo drove the Kouros-sponsored C8 into 8th place. [Photo: Courtesy of LAT.]

At Le Mans in 1986, Henri Pescarolo, Christian Danner and Dieter Quester raced the number 62 C8 but they were out after seven hours when the gearbox failed. [Photo: Courtesy of LAT.]

came from Michelin instead of Goodyear and several good results (but no wins!) were recorded. The car did, however, sit on pole at the Spa-Francorchamps 1000 kms race.

Much was expected of the team at Le Mans and Johnny Dumfries set a lap record and ran as high as fourth before the gearbox wilted. Henri Pescarolo made makeshift repairs to the

The Kouros-backed Sauber-Mercedes C8 in the pits at Le Mans during the night. [Photo: Courtesy of LAT.]

universal joint, which had failed and got the C9 back to the pits, only to find that the team, despairing of him re-appearing, had packed up! The team came back and fixed the Sauber but the gearbox failed later on this car too.

At the end of the season, Kouros withdrew their support from Peter Sauber's team, but Mercedes stepped in, using one of their companies, AEG Olympia office automation systems, to sponsor the Sauber team. Additionally, Mercedes also helped Sauber develop the Hewland VGC gearbox, using components made at Staffs Silent Gears in England. Four factory technicians now attended each race in the Sauber pits, looking after the engines.

At the Monza 1000 kms race of 1986, John Neilsen and Henri Pescarolo took 9th place in their Sauber-Mercedes C8. [Photo: Courtesy of LAT.]

[Photo: Courtesy of LAT.]

Chapter 2

Mercedes Engine Development

As we have seen, Heini Mader's tuning firm had substantially developed the engine used in the Sauber-Mercedes C9 before the Mercedes-Benz engine development team, headed by Dr. Hermann Hiereth, took the development back, in-house. Over the winter of 1987-88, Hiereth's team worked further on the M117 HL engine and a closer look at this unit will help the reader appreciate just why it out-performed the opposition, both in power and fuel consumption.

First of all, the M117's aluminum crankcase was taken from the production line of the engine blocks intended for the 500SL passenger cars that used the engine. Then, the specially selected blocks were sent to Mahle, the noted piston and liner maker, for the bores to be treated with Nikasil, which did away with the need for a separate steel cylinder liner. Mahle had performed the same service for Porsche 911/930 cylinders for many years.

The M117 engine block had sides that extended below the crankshaft centerline, to give more strength in this critical area. Vertical bolts were used to locate the crankshaft bearings. The special magnesium dry-sump was stressed to accept chassis loads and the engine was semi-stressed in this area, the heads being used as auxiliary mounting points. Beneath the production valve covers, the valve gear was mounted directly onto the heads, each cylinder secured to the block via six headbolts.

The crankshaft was of forged steel, a two-plane design fitted with a harmonic damper, and the standard-size 7.25 inch AP racing clutch was surrounded by the starter ring. Titanium connecting rods were attached to the Mahle aluminum pistons, which were secured by a steel gudgeon pin with circlips at either end. A jet of oil from beneath the piston crown cooled these pistons. Each piston carried three cast iron rings, supplied from TRW in America.

Oddly, for a racing engine, the M117 HL's compression ratio was less than the road-going engine's 10:1 equivalent. Of course, this was because the engine used in the C9 employed turbocharging, artificially increasing the compression ratio when in action. The two valves per cylinder of the M117 HL were placed one behind the other in the combustion chamber, with the sparkplug situated opposite. A dish in the piston crown gave the necessary reduction in compression ratio. The steel Nimonic tipped valves ran in bronze guides and the exhaust valves were filled with sodium, to aid cooling. There were twin springs fitted to each valve. The production valve gear was still used on the race engine but the hydraulic operation had been dispensed with, mechanical adjustment taking its place.

The hollow camshafts were supported in five bearings each and were built up in sections whilst being heated. When cool, these camshaft parts shrank to fit its next section. The camshafts were chain-driven from the crankshaft, still using the normal production chain with a tensioner being fitted. The oil pressure pump was also

The lightly-turbocharged M117 two-valve Mercedes V8 engine. [Photo: Courtesy of LAT.]

driven from the nose of the crankshaft, but by a separate sprocket. The five scavenge pumps (three for the dry-sump system, two for the turbochargers), were belt-driven from a pulley, again mounted on the nose of the crankshaft. Another pulley drove the water pump and the alternator. Enlarged water passages in the block and heads gave twice as much coolant throughput in the race engine as in the production version.

The fuel injection system used injectors screwed directly into the heads (one per cylinder), instead of into the intake ports. The switch from the previous Bosch Motronic 1.2 system had allowed one extra injector, used only for full throttle activation, to be discarded.

With the installation of the Motronic 1.7 engine management system, a switch from the previous Bosch CD system to a multi-coil system, which took its impulses from a camshaft and flywheel sensor, was made. With one coil firing two cylinders, each sparkplug fired twice each stroke, to no noticeable detriment.

Each KKK turbocharger blew through its own air-to air intercooler and the turbochargers themselves featured an electronically controlled wastegate, controlled by the electronic control unit. This ECU "brain", took its messages from the crankshaft, camshaft, charge air pressure, air and exhaust gas pressures, fuel temperature and pressure and turbocharger rpm. In America, co-incidentally, the Electramotive Company of El Segundo had just come up with an electronically controlled wastegate of their own, which would give them almost the same degree of success in IMSA racing as Sauber-Mercedes was to enjoy in Europe in the next two years. The driver was still in charge of just how much turbo boost was used, however, via a control in the cockpit.

These Mercedes-Benz race engines took two engineers a week to strip and rebuild back at the factory. Qualifying boost was 1.2 bar absolute at which pressure maximum power was stated at some 800 bhp at 7000 rpm. For the race itself, driver instructions called for a maximum of 6,500 rpm to be used, except, perhaps, for overtaking. Torque was quoted at 570 foot pounds at 4,750 rpm and was a very flat band for a racing engine, extending from 3,000 to 8,000 rpm. It was this enormous torque that was to give the Sauber-Mercedes such an advantage in exiting corners.

Chapter 3

[Photo: Courtesy of LAT.]

Mercedes in 1988

The afternoon of the 12th January, 1988 saw Mercedes' backing for the Sauber Group C program formally ratified by the Directors of Daimler-Benz. Dr. Werner Niefer had become Deputy Chairman of Mercedes-Benz and strongly backed the Mercedes return to the race circuits of Europe. After an absence of thirty-three years, Mercedes were officially back in racing.

At this time, although the FIA managed the World Championship for Sports Prototypes (WS-PC), it was, in effect, only a European Championship with occasional rounds being held in Japan and Mexico.

America had its own IMSA (International Motor Sport Association) Camel GT Championship, which had different rules to the FIA's, particularly where the fuel consumption regulations of Group C were concerned. John Bishop, the President of IMSA, had declined to institute these regulations, fearing that the American public would not stand a formula where the leading car backed off to get to the finish. In hindsight, bearing in mind the WS-PC's demise, Bishop was probably right.

However, Mercedes saw the fuel challenge in a different light, reasoning that the electronic engine management improvements necessary for Group C cars would aid the general efficiency of their road cars, as well as the associated publicity that Mercedes participation in motor racing would bring.

For 1988, Mercedes hired Jean-Louis Schlesser, Jochen Mass and Mauro Baldi to drive for Sauber-Mercedes. Jochen Mass remembered: "Well, Peter Sauber called and I went to drive for him. Of course, the fact that Mercedes was doing the engines helped a lot!"

"The C9 was a great car. A league different and faster than a Porsche 962. It was very demanding and, to begin with, nothing was sorted properly. Later on, the aerodynamics, tires, dampers, everything changed and developed."

Jochen Mass: "Leo Ress started to develop the Sauber, by concentrating on the dampers. We changed over from Bilstein to Sachs and the improvement was dramatic."

Leo Ress: "The Bilstein dampers had too much friction in them and they also suffered from a lack of development at the time. The Sachs dampers improved matters greatly."

Dave Price went to work for Sauber-Mercedes as their Team Manager: "It was a funny situation, really," recalled Dave. "Peter Sauber didn't speak English as well then as he does now. He asked Max Welti to ask me to join the team while we were at Silverstone in 1987. Max speaks about ten languages, by the way!"

With just a single car, but now with official Mercedes factory backing, the Sauber team started 1988 on a triumphant note, winning the first race held at Jerez. Jochen Mass, Jean-Louis Schlesser and Mauro Baldi beat the three TWR Jaguar XJR-9's entered by 20 seconds over nearly five hundred miles of racing. [Photo: Courtesy of LAT.]

"So Max became in charge of administration and movement and I ran the cars at the race weekends. There were only about fifteen people in the team at that time. I'd been working for Richard Lloyd with the 962 and could see that the Sauber was quick but struggling with reliability and their pitstops were bad. In those days, you could be team manager and engineer one of the cars and this is what I did in 1988. The drivers were the best bunch that you could hope for – I ran the Baldi/Schlesser car in 1988 and the Baldi/Acheson car in 1989. Schlesser asked me if I would go back to

Dave Price (at left) was the Team Manager for Sauber-Mercedes in 1989. Jean-Louis Schlesser suits up whilst Jochen Mass discusses tactics with Dave Price. [Photo: Courtesy of LAT.]

his car in 1989 but I had my hands full with everything going on by then."

The Mercedes involvement got off to a great start, as the C9/87 Sauber-Mercedes won at Jerez in Spain: Jean-Louis Schlesser, Jochen Mass and Mauro Baldi piloting the winning car. The C9/88 cars were still being made, and so the singleton C9/87 had been upgraded from the 1987 version, particularly in the engine and gearbox department. Another C9/87 was used as the practice and qualifying car.

TWR Jaguar started the season as Champions, and were somewhat surprised when the Sauber-Mercedes claimed pole position at Jerez by almost two seconds. Certainly, the huge low-end torque of the Mercedes V8 helped around the twisty nature of the Jerez circuit. Jochen Mass again: "You know, I would say that the TWR-Jaguars had the upper edge on us aerodynamically at the start of 1988. I believe that we had the better engines and they had their problems, as well as us."

"The Sauber team in 1988 was composed of old hands in racing where the drivers were concerned, and now we had Mercedes as, effectively, our engine supplier. I had been in Formula One, and there is a great deal of difference between a sprint race and settling down for six hours in a thousand kilometer race. Of course, any of us could turn out a fast qualifying lap, but when you realize that we had to run to a limited fuel allocation, you can see that running to a steady program was more important than flying around."

At the start of the Jerez race, the Jaguar of Martin Brundle and Eddie Cheever had taken the lead, leaving its two teammates to fight with the Mercedes. After just sixty laps, the "cats" were first through third, with the Sauber-Mercedes holding fourth place. Andy Wallace had to take avoiding action when lapping a C2 car, and the subsequent trip into the countryside forced him to stop to get the radiator inlets cleared out. The Sauber was now third. Two laps later, Jan Lammers came on the radio to tell the crew that his Jaguar was stuck in fifth gear. Mass was up to second place now.

Ahead of Mass was Martin Brundle with a seven second lead, but almost before Mass could start to make a dent on the leading car's advantage, Brundle called into the pits and Eddie Cheever took over. Cheever still had the advantage but shortly afterwards his car lost fourth and fifth gears and the battle for the lead was effectively over: Schlesser, Baldi and Mass cruising to the flag to take victory.

At Jarama, just one week later, the same Sauber-Mercedes C9/87 (chassis number 02) took pole position again, but not by as much of a margin as they had done at Jerez. This time, only .6 seconds separated the lone Sauber-Mercedes from the first of the three TWR-Jaguar XJR-9s: that of Jan Lammers and Johnny Dumfries. That said, it should be pointed out that the Jaguars had

(Continued on page 22)

Sauber-Mercedes

Sauber C9-87.02, driven by Jean-Louis Schlesser and Mauro Baldi was narrowly beaten at Jarama by Eddie Cheever and Martin Brundle in the 7-liter engined Jaguar XJR-9. The Sauber had taken pole position but was forced to pit twice for new Michelin tires, against the Jaguars single stop for harder compound Dunlops. [Photo: Courtesy of LAT.]

*Mauro Baldi.
[Photo: Courtesy of LAT.]*

tested before at this Spanish circuit, whereas the Sauber-Mercedes had not.

That Jaguar won this time was primarily down to tires, the Dunlops of the winning Jaguar allowing the TWR-run car to take only one pit stop, whereas the Michelins of the Sauber-Mercedes required two changes. Late on in the race, Schlesser was holding on to third place with his tires rapidly going off when Johnny Dumfries, holding second place, went off and became stuck in a gravel trap, thus promoting the Sauber-Mercedes to second place.

Jochen Mass again: "Michelin are a great company, but we had problems with them. Their tires' sidewalls weren't strong enough to take the loadings that the Sauber-Mercedes put through them with its

Once again, Sauber fielded a single car at Monza in April, the same car that had been run at Jerez and Jarama. Although it took pole position and led the early laps, the Sauber was forced to turn down the boost to make it to the finish and was beaten into second place by the more fuel-efficient Jaguar XJR-9 of Brundle and Cheever. [Photo: Courtesy of LAT.]

downforce and they went off quite quickly. Michelin wanted Sauber to design a new car that would not have as much downforce as we already had, but of course, that would have taken us down the wrong road. We did win Le Mans with them, so they weren't that bad! But when we went to Goodyears, they were much better, stiffer tires."

Almost a month passed before the Jaguars and the Sauber-Mercedes faced each other again, this time at Monza for the 1000 kms race. It had become obvious during the first three races that Porsche, whose 956/962 design was now some six years old, could not get a look in against the more modern designs of TWR-Jaguar and Sauber.

After dealing with a fuel specification problem (a tanker had to come from Germany with the correct specification fuel), the teams went out to qualify and it was no surprise to see the Sauber-Mercedes topping the time sheets yet again. There was a surprise, however, in the second car on the front of the grid. This was a Joest-run Porsche 962 and behind it in third place was another 962, this one a Walter Brun entered car. The first Jaguar was in fourth place.

Monza is a fast track, meaning that the more economic Jaguar had an advantage here that it used to the full, Martin Brundle and Eddie Cheever lapping the second-placed Sauber-Mercedes on its way to victory. Porsche 962s filled the next four places but it has to be said that the turbocharged cars had suffered in the fuel consumption stakes in Italy.

On May 8th, the Autosport 1000 Kilometers race took place at Silverstone. Over 35,000 fans turned out to watch the Jaguar/Sauber battle and, once again, the Sauber-Mercedes took pole position, over one and a half seconds faster than the second-placed TWR Jaguar of Martin Brundle and Eddie Cheever. Mercedes had brought along their usual C9-87-02, plus a new C9 (chassis number-03) and another C9/87, which was used as the "T" car. In practice on the Friday, the Mercedes engineers tried new electronics in the engine management system but this resulted in too much boost being applied in the engines, both of which blew up. The mechanics were faced with two engine changes overnight.

Heavy rain stopped just two hours before the start of the race and thankfully did not re-occur. The whole field chose slicks and the first part of the race saw Eddie Cheever in the leading Jaguar having a monstrous dice with the two Sauber-Mercedes. Cheever then handed over to Martin Brundle who, with the two Sauber-Mercedes drivers watching their fuel read-out meters, pulled out a thirty-second lead on the Swiss-German cars. At the flag, it was the TWR-Jaguar to take the laurels in front of a cheering home crowd.

And then it was time for the big one: Le Mans. Jaguar entered five cars in their third attempt to win the classic endurance race and Sauber-Mercedes entered three

The first lap at Monza with the Kouros-sponsored Sauber leading the field. Right behind the Sauber is the Porsche 962C of Oscar Larrauri and Massimo Sigala that finished in third place. [Photo: Courtesy of LAT.]

C9s, including a "T", or practice car. Their participation in this year's race was brief.

Klaus Niedzwiedz had a rear tire blowout on the fastest part of the course on Wednesday evening, when he was travelling at well over 220 mph. Thankfully, he managed to keep the car off the barriers and crawl back to the pits. After much discussion and a failure by Michelin to reassure the team that the same thing could not happen again, the Sauber-Mercedes team withdrew from the race the next morning, fearful of another repetition of 1955, when a Mercedes 300SLR had catapulted into the crowds, killing 80 people.

It later transpired that the TWR-Jaguar's Goodyear tires also suffered from overheating, but they, being of radial construction, were better able to cope with it. In the race itself, TWR Jaguar won after a race-long scrap with the factory Shell-sponsored Porsche 962s.

The Czech Republic was the next round of the WS-PC and saw Sauber bring two C9s into the fray. In qualifying, the two Sauber-Mercedes claimed the front row and, worse still for TWR-Jaguar, a Joest-Porsche 962 took the fourth slot, beating the second Jaguar back to the third row.

At the start, both Sauber-Mercedes leapt into an early lead but on lap ten, Baldi pitted with a punctured left rear tire. This incident put him back into sixth place, fighting oversteer and battling with the Jaguars and Joest-Porsches. Schlesser and Mass ran out the winners, the two TWR-Jaguars placing second and third, and James Weaver and Mauro Baldi finally managing to overcome Bob Wollek and "John Winter's" Porsche. The first four all finished on the same lap.

Jean-Louis Schlesser.
[Photo: Courtesy of LAT.]

At Brands Hatch for the 1000 kms race, the C9s and the Joest-962s set their times in between showers whilst the TWR Jaguars only seemed to go out in the wet. This put the TWR Jaguars back into fourth place at the start.

Jaguar were lucky here as the Sauber-Mercedes took off into an early lead, with Klaus Ludwig's Joest-entered Porsche 962 scrapping with them. On lap eight, Steve Hynes, driving a C2 spun when trying to give room to the charging leaders and his Tiga collected Mass' C9, which was heavily damaged in the resulting crash. Baldi's Sauber was forced to pit for new tires, as he had spun in avoiding the accident. This elevated the TWR-Jaguars into the second two places until the Joest 962 was forced to slow with fuel consumption problems. It looked as if this would give TWR a one-two finish until a dashboard fire put the Lammers/Dumfries car out on lap 212, leaving the Nielson/Brundle/Wallace XJR-9 with the win.

As at the previous Nürburgring race, conditions were very bad, the rain forcing the organizers to reduce the length of the race to six hours. Just about everyone had problems, the Schlesser/Mass C9 retiring with a broken rear suspension wishbone, Lammers and Brundle had a puncture and bad tires, and Baldi and Johansson had a dragging clutch and oil on their windshield. Nevertheless, at the end, it was the C9 of Baldi and Johansson that ran out the winner with Lammers and Brundle taking the necessary second place to make TWR-Jaguar the 1988 WS-PC Champions.

Having taken the team title, TWR-Jaguar celebrated in fine style at Mount Fuji on October 9th as Martin Brundle, TWR's lead driver, won the Driver's Championship too. The 1000 kilometers of Fuji saw an excellent entry, no less than nine official factory teams taking part. Nissan and Toyota were prominent in the field, and indeed, it was a Nissan that gave the hardest time in qualifying to the pole-sitting FromA Porsche 962 of Hideki Okada. The Nissan R88C was only hundredths of a second slower and the C9s and TWR-Jaguars were well back on the grid.

It was a different story come the race itself, the struggle between the Jaguars and the Sauber-Mercedes hotting up, with the occasional Porsche 962 trying to get a look-in. Martin Brundle and Eddie Cheever did all that was expected of them to win, but the C9s suffered misfortune when a faulty electronic sensor lost turbo boost and four laps and, effectively, put Schlesser's title hopes beyond recall. The other C9 had the misfortune to suffer a tire failure at 190 mph at the end of the main straight and finished up in the barriers with the driver, Philippe Streif, thankfully unhurt.

Jochen Mass.
[Photo: Courtesy of LAT.]

Even though both the drivers and the team Championship had been resolved in favor of Martin Brundle and TWR-Jaguar respectively, Sauber-Mercedes still sent cars half-way around the World to Australia to contest the final round of the Championship, held at Sandown Park, near Melbourne.

The AEG-sponsored Sauber-Mercedes C9s finished first and second, the TWR-Jaguars suffering from fuel consumption problems in third place and being able to do nothing about the Saubers as they controlled the race.

The Sauber-Mercedes team finished the season in second place to the TWR-Jaguar team but to anyone who watched the last few races of 1988, it was clear that the Swiss-German team had found a winning combination. With the continuous development that Mercedes were able to put behind their part of the equation, TWR-Jaguar knew that they faced a tough season to come.

CHAPTER 4

The 1989 version, now in the Mercedes "Silver Arrow" colors of the Sauber C9. [Photo: Courtesy of LAT.]

Mercedes Engine Development 1988-1989

O ver the winter of 1988 to 1989, the Mercedes-Benz engineers, under the direction of Dr. Ing. Hermann Hiereth, went back to the drawing board to re-design the top end of their successful M117 HL V-8 engine. Rightly reasoning that a four-valve per cylinder layout would be volumetrically more efficient than the two-valve per cylinder setup (and, therefore, better suited to the Group C formula, which rewarded good fuel efficiency), the engineers, amongst them Withalm, Bachrens and Muller, designed, produced and developed the new heads in short order.

Still chain-driven from the nose of the crankshaft, the four overhead camshafts now each drove two cam lobes per cylinder. There was now an ideally situated centrally positioned sparkplug that fired into a combustion chamber with squish bands on either side of the new, shallowly dished piston. The compression ratio was still a nominal 8.5:1.

The 38 mm diameter inlet valves were inclined at 23 degrees from the head's centerline, whilst the 33 mm diameter exhaust valves were at 14.5 degrees. All thirty-two valves were sodium filled. The Mahle-supplied, built-up camshafts were of the same type as the M117 HL but now each cylinder's combustion chamber was secured by four, instead of six, bolts.

Bore and stroke were still 96.5 x 85.00 mm, giving a total engine capacity of 4,973 cc. One big distinction between the two and four valve engines was the height of the blocks, that of the M119 HL was 20 mm lower at the top deck than the previous M117 HL. This managed to offset the extra weight of the new heads and to lower the center of gravity of the engine in the chassis. As an aside, it is worth noting that Jaguar also used four-valve per cylinder technology in their later TWR-XJR's, but the added weight upset that car's handling quite dramatically to begin with.

The titanium connecting rods of the M119 HL at 155 mm were shorter than those of the M117 HL. With the new heads, pistons, connecting rods and crankshaft fitted, the M119 achieved a 30% reduction in rotational inertia over the previous M117 HL. Weight without intercoolers was now 467 pounds, slightly increased from that of the M117 HL, but with the 1989 minimum weight limit of the Group C1 cars to 1,985 pounds, this was not a problem.

The power output of the M119 HL engine was substantially increased over that of the M117 HL. The 1989 engine could deliver 925 bhp in qualifying trim but what was more important, could deliver 770 bhp in full race trim, as against the previous 660 bhp available from the M117 HL.

The improvement in torque delivery was even more marked. At 3,000 rpm, the

The 1989 version of the M117 Mercedes V8. [Photo: Courtesy of LAT.]

Sauber-Mercedes

Another view of the 1989 version of Mercedes' M119 V8. Note the carbon fiber plenum chamber and the horizontally mounted read damper/coil springs. [Photo: Courtesy of LAT.]

The cockpit of the 1989 Sauber-Mercedes C9 with telemetry being downloaded. Note the Bosch Motronic unit in the passenger compartment. [Photo: Courtesy of LAT.]

M119 HL delivered 550 foot pounds of torque, as against the old engine's 515 foot pounds. Even at 7,000 rpm, the M119 HL was still providing some 550 foot pounds, the M117 HL 512 foot pounds.

The most important feature of the new engine's performance was its capacity to provide more power at the same boost level over the previous M117 HL, but without using any extra fuel. This was primarily due to the better, more efficient combustion chamber shape that gave 304 p.s.i. brake mean effective pressure (bmep), as against the M117 HL's 284 p.s.i.

Sauber and Mercedes had agreed to build a composite tub for use in 1989 for a new car to be called the C11, but this project was shelved when it was discovered that neither had the experience necessary to produce it in 1989. For 1990, the story would be different.

The rear suspension of the C9/89 was revised from that used in 1988. Now, the track-control arm was pivoted directly to the chassis, instead of the upper front wishbone, thus reducing the stress on the wishbone pivot. Where the bodywork was concerned, the C9/89 benefited from having the space behind the lower front wheel filled-in to fare the airflow better, and the rear wing-post was faired-in. A carbon-carbon clutch was used for the sprint races.

Brembo supplied fourteen inch carbon rotors, four-pot calipers and pads, each capable of lasting a complete 480-kilometer race distance. Because of the lightness of these brakes, the car proved easier to drive, as well as stopping in a shorter distance. When used frequently, as at short, twisty circuits, these brakes had a tendency to glaze, either failing to stop the C9/89, or becoming too "juddery", reducing the driver's confidence in them.

For Le Mans, in its quest for reliability over the long distance, the team reverted to steel brakes and clutch. A spool, instead of a limited-slip differential was fitted, allowing the car to be driven back to the pits for repairs if a half-shaft or universal joint broke out on the circuit. Fifth gear here was half as wide again as the "normal" one used, first gear correspondingly narrower. Not only this, but the engines were tested on a Le Mans "cycle" on the dynamometer for 40 hours, and the cars completed a simulated 24-hour test with two cars at Paul Ricard in March 1989.

Surprisingly, during the first tests, the C9/89, with its new four-valve heads, proved to be no faster than the C9/88. This was put down to the extra weight (forty-five pounds) of the four-valve heads upsetting the handling and a program of weight reduction and, more significantly, a lowering of the center of gravity was undertaken. When this had been accomplished, the C9/89 proved to be faster than its predecessor and, most notably, showed a marked improvement in fuel consumption.

Dave Price, the 1989 Team Manager, stated: "We (DPS) built the carbon chassis for the C11s. I remember that we sent Mercedes a lot of parts for them. Mercedes then needed to carve some engine weight off the top of their four-valve engine and so we made a plenum chamber out of carbon and sent it to them. They thought that it wouldn't be as strong as the aluminum one they were using. Of course, the turbochargers were only using about 0.8 bar maximum for a race and so Mercedes tested our new carbon plenum. They told us later that they had to stress it to 7.0 plus bar before it failed!"

Jochen Mass in the cockpit of a C9.
[Photo: Courtesy of LAT.]

Due to the increased efficiency of the new four-valve heads, the C9/89 proved to need less boost than the two-valve engine had needed for any given power output. This made the car easier to drive and kinder to the tires than the C9/88. However, the rear suspension still had scope for further improvement.

[Photo: Courtesy of LAT.]

Chapter 5

Sauber-Mercedes in 1989

In 1989, the FIA instituted a rule to force those manufacturers who only participated at Le Mans to enter every WSPC race on the calendar but one, on pain of a $250,000 fine. At once, this forced Nissan and Toyota into the ranks of the contenders. The FIA also began a two year transitional period in 1989, wishing to introduce a 3.5-liter, naturally aspirated "lightweight" formula in 1991. In 1989, the "old" turbo cars were forced to weigh a minimum of 900 kgs, whilst the "lightweights" could run at 750 kgs. There were no fuel limitations for the 3.5-liter cars either, whereas the old turbo cars still had to run to a limited fuel allocation.

These measures forced Sauber-Mercedes to look at producing what became the C291 with its flat-12 engine. However, for 1989, Mercedes reasoned that the C9, with some development, was quite sufficient to see off the new breed of lightweight cars.

1989 was also the year that the Mercedes backing of Peter Sauber's team became more obvious. The cars were now turned out in Mercedes silver as the "Silver Arrows", with the Mercedes three-pointed star prominent on the front of the C9/88. The principal difference from the C9/88 was the four-valve per cylinder layout of the V8 engine.

For the factory, Jochen Neerpasch became Competitions Director with Max Welti, as Team Manager, hiring Dave Price, the accomplished English team manager to help run the team. "Pricey", as he is known around the race world, brought Bob Bell with him as Jean-Louis Schlesser's race engineer.

Bob Bell: "Sauber were a fantastic team to work for. Schlesser and Jochen Mass were a great, complementary team. 'Schless' would qualify the car usually, but I remember that, at Jarama, 'Schless' wasn't well, so Jochen qualified the car. We still finished up on pole!"

For drivers, the accomplished Jean-Louis Schlesser and Mauro Baldi were retained as the designated lead drivers, with Ulsterman Kenny Acheson pairing with Baldi and Jochen Mass relieving Schlesser.

Kenny Acheson: "I'd first of all driven the Sauber-Mercedes the year before at Mount Fuji, and that really landed me the 1989 drive. I had been slated to drive at Le Mans also but the tire problem meant that I

Previous page: The Sauber-Mercedes C9 of 1989. This is the winning car at Le Mans driven by Jochen Mass, Stanley Dickens and Manuel Reuter. [Photo: Courtesy of the Daimler/Chrysler Archives.]

Kenny Acheson gave superb support to Mauro Baldi, often leading races but dropping back to team orders. [Photo: Courtesy of LAT.]

didn't get to drive, which was probably a good job, because the cars were too slow that year."

"I learned a lot in 1989. Mercedes certainly knew how to do things the right way. In my judgement, the Sauber was the class of the field in 1989, and that was why we won so many races. The only real problem was the tires. Michelin is a fantastic Company, probably the best in motor racing, but in 1989, their tires went off quite quickly and made the C9 want to oversteer."

Bob Bell: "Poor Kenny never got enough seat time in the cars. Mauro Baldi wanted to do too much driving, in my opinion."

These drivers had their own comfort seen to in the C9/89. An opening in the nose took in cool air, whilst holes in the roof encouraged a through-flow of this cooling air, significantly lowering the cockpit temperature. Thirty pounds of lead weight was added to the sponsons to bring the minimum weight up to the now-required 900 kilograms.

The WSPC began at Suzuka in 1989, on April 9th and the Sauber/Daimler-Benz team were out-qualified by the Toyotas, who took the front row, and Jan Lammers' "old" TWR-Jaguar XJR-9, as the team's new turbo V6 engined car was not ready. Come race day, Jochen Mass came down with a viral infection, which affected his eyesight and so Kenny

(Continued on page 42)

Magnificent sight (and sound!). The two Sauber-Mercedes ran nose to tail at Suzuka's opening race and C9-88.04, that of Schlesser and Baldi, beat the C9-88.03 of Kenny Acheson by just a small gap. [Photo: Courtesy of LAT.]

WORLD CHAMPIONS – THE GROUP C CARS

Opening lap of the race at Dijon with the Sauber-Mercedes C9 of Schlesser and Mass already in the lead. Behind the Sauber-Mercedes are Porsche 962Cs, a Nissan R89C, TWR Jaguar XJR-9 and a Spice SE 88. [Photo: Courtesy of LAT.]

Sauber-Mercedes

Acheson elected to drive solo as the events had now been reduced from the old 1000 kms length to 480 kms. Acheson also suffered from the C9 having qualified in thirtieth position, as it had done very few laps in the rainy qualifying session.

At Dijon, Jean-Louis Schlesser and Jochen Mass shared Sauber C9-88.04 but, despite having taken pole position, could do nothing about Reinhold Joest's new "sprint" Porsche 962 (chassis number 962C011). The Joest car had Goodyear tires, which suited the circuit better than the Michelin-shod Saubers. [Photo: Courtesy of LAT.]

Through one of the chicanes on the Mulsanne straight goes one of the team of three Sauber-Mercedes on their way to victory at Le Mans in 1989. This is the C9 that finished in second place, driven by Mauro Baldi, Kenny Acheson and Gianfranco Brancatelli. [Photo: Courtesy of LAT.]

At the start, Schlesser caught and passed the two lead Toyotas and led the first lap by four seconds until Paolo Barilla, driving one of the Toyotas, turned up the boost and passed Schlesser, to the enormous delight of the huge crowd. It did not last, Barilla spinning the Toyota three laps later and pitting for new tires. Wollek's Porsche 962 now took second place whilst Kenny Acheson, pacing himself carefully, steadily moved through the field. The Jaguars appeared not to be in contention, their fuel consumption forcing them into endurance mode in what was, compared with the last year, a sprint race.

Mauro Baldi took over from Schlesser and stayed ahead of the Ogawa/Barilla Toyota. The first pit-stops had put the Wollek/Jelinski Porsche down into third place. Acheson now hunted down and passed the Toyota and then passed Frank Jelinski. At Acheson's fuel stop, he got out in the lead as he did not need as much fuel as the sister team car, having run at such a reserved pace early on.

After requests from Max Welti had failed to make Kenny Acheson move over for the more experienced team leaders, Dave Price got on the radio and Acheson reluctantly moved over to surrender what would have been his maiden victory, first time out in the C9. Nevertheless, it was a great start to the year for Mercedes, with their principal rivals, TWR-Jaguar, not being able to finish higher than fifth.

There was now a gap of several weeks before the next race at Dijon and the FIA organized an open test session, where the Sauber-Mercedes topped the time sheets with, surprisingly, a reversal of fortune for the faster Porsche 962s, their pace being almost comparable. Toyota were also seen as being on the pace.

In qualifying at Dijon, Schlesser put the Sauber-Mercedes on pole with the Toyota driven by Johnny Dumfries coming second fastest ahead of the Bell/Needell Porsche 962 and the Joest 962 of Wollek and Jelinski closing out the front two rows. The TWR Jaguars could do no better than seventh and ninth.

The race turned out a surprise victor. Although Schlesser and Baldi (the lead drivers for, respectively, Mass and Acheson) led at the start, Bob Wollek in the Joest Porsche 962, and Frank Jelinski, his co-driver, were not to be denied and ruthlessly forced their way past any car ahead of them to take and keep the lead. In this, they were assisted by the fact that the Sauber's Michelins were wearing out at a faster rate than the Joest car's Goodyears were.

With the victory decided, there was a sharp tussle between Schlesser and Baldi, the Italian having caught the sister car on the last lap, but Jean-Louis held off Mauro to take the extra points that would count towards the Drivers' Championship.

WORLD CHAMPIONS – THE GROUP C CARS

Unsung heroes. Sauber and Mercedes technicians hard at work at Le Mans in 1989, preparing what was to be the winning car for the battle to come. [Photo: Courtesy of LAT.]

First lap and two Mercedes are already leading the 1989 Le Mans 24-Hour race, followed by two Porsche 962C's. [Photo: Courtesy of LAT.]

The organizers of the Le Mans 24-Hour race had failed to reach agreement over television rights with the FIA and so the French classic was dropped from the WSPC. This had no effect, whatsoever on the entry list, all teams knowing that Le Mans alone counts for more publicity, prestige and respect than all the World Championship races put together.

Sauber-Mercedes entered four cars, one used as a spare. The extra drivers for the team were Jean-Pierre Jabouille, Alain Cudini, Gianfranco Brancatelli, Manuel Reuter and Stanley Dickens. There were three drivers allocated to each car. The cars themselves appeared to differ little from their usual race bodywork, except that their

Pitstop time for the winning Mercedes during the Le Mans 24-Hours race of 1989. [Photo: Courtesy of LAT.]

rear wings were noticeably mounted higher and further back.

The reality was different. Typical of Mercedes' thoroughness, the Le Mans project had entailed wind-tunnel testing of the C9/89 from as far back as November 1988. At the front, the wheel arch louvers had been removed. An insert was fitted

Battered but unbowed. Seen in the latter stages of the race at Le Mans, this Sauber-Mercedes displays evidence of contact with slower cars but still went on to take the win. [Photo: Courtesy of LAT.]

to make a shallower underbody venturi tunnel. The new wing had a narrower chord and only one element. The downforce to drag ratio went down from 4.0 to 3.0 to 1. This new bodywork had been tested at the Michelin truck-testing circuit, as were the tires necessary to cope with the 237.5 mph achieved in that test.

Two of the C9s filled the front row in qualifying with two of the TWR-Jaguars occupying the second row. For Porsche, Reinhold Joest's team fielded a very strong three-car entry, with Bob Wollek and Hans Stuck sharing the fastest car.

Having won in 1988, TWR-Jaguar were back in force for Le Mans, entering four cars and a battle royal between the English and German teams was expected. The huge audience was not to be disappointed.

Although Mauro Baldi led at the start, Davy Jones, driving a double stint in his Jaguar, got past

Driver change and refueling pit stop for the victorious Mercedes C9. [Photo: Courtesy of LAT]

Superb shot of the Baldi/Acheson Sauber-Mercedes C9-87.02, with Mauro Baldi at the wheel, at Jarama where they placed fifth. The sister car, driven by Schlesser and Mass, was the outright winner. [Photo: Courtesy of LAT.]

him and held the lead after the first round of pitstops. Bob Wollek was in pursuit, having passed Baldi. Derek Daly took over from Jones but the TWR-Jaguar then had difficulty with the differential and finally retired in the night when a valve dropped into a cylinder.

All of these problems for the other teams put the Wollek/Stuck Porsche into the lead, where it was shortly joined by its

At Brands Hatch, the Sauber-Mercedes finished first and third, Mauro Baldi and Kenny Acheson winning, whilst the sister car of Jean-Louis Schlesser and Jochen Mass could only mange third after a rear tire threw it's tread, damaging their suspension. [Photo: Courtesy of LAT.]

Brands Hatch again, and the Mauro Baldi/Kenny Acheson car sweeps through Bottom bend. [Photo: Courtesy of LAT.]

sister car, driven by Frank Jelinski, Pierre-Henri Raphanel and Louis Krages ("John Winter"). However, the fastest TWR-Jaguar, that driven by Jan Lammers, Patrick Tambay and Andrew Gilbert-Scott, was creeping up the order as was the third Sauber-Mercedes of Mass/Reuter and Dickens.

During the early morning, the fastest 962, the Joest entry, dropped to fifth position with a cracked water pipe and Tambay's

Changeover time. Jochen Mass waits to relieve Jean-Louis Schlesser at a pitstop at the Nürburgring, during their triumphant run there in C9-88-05. Although the Sauber-Mercedes won in the end due to its fuel economy, the new Lola-Nissan R89C gave it a hard run, and led most of the race. [Photo: Courtesy of LAT.]

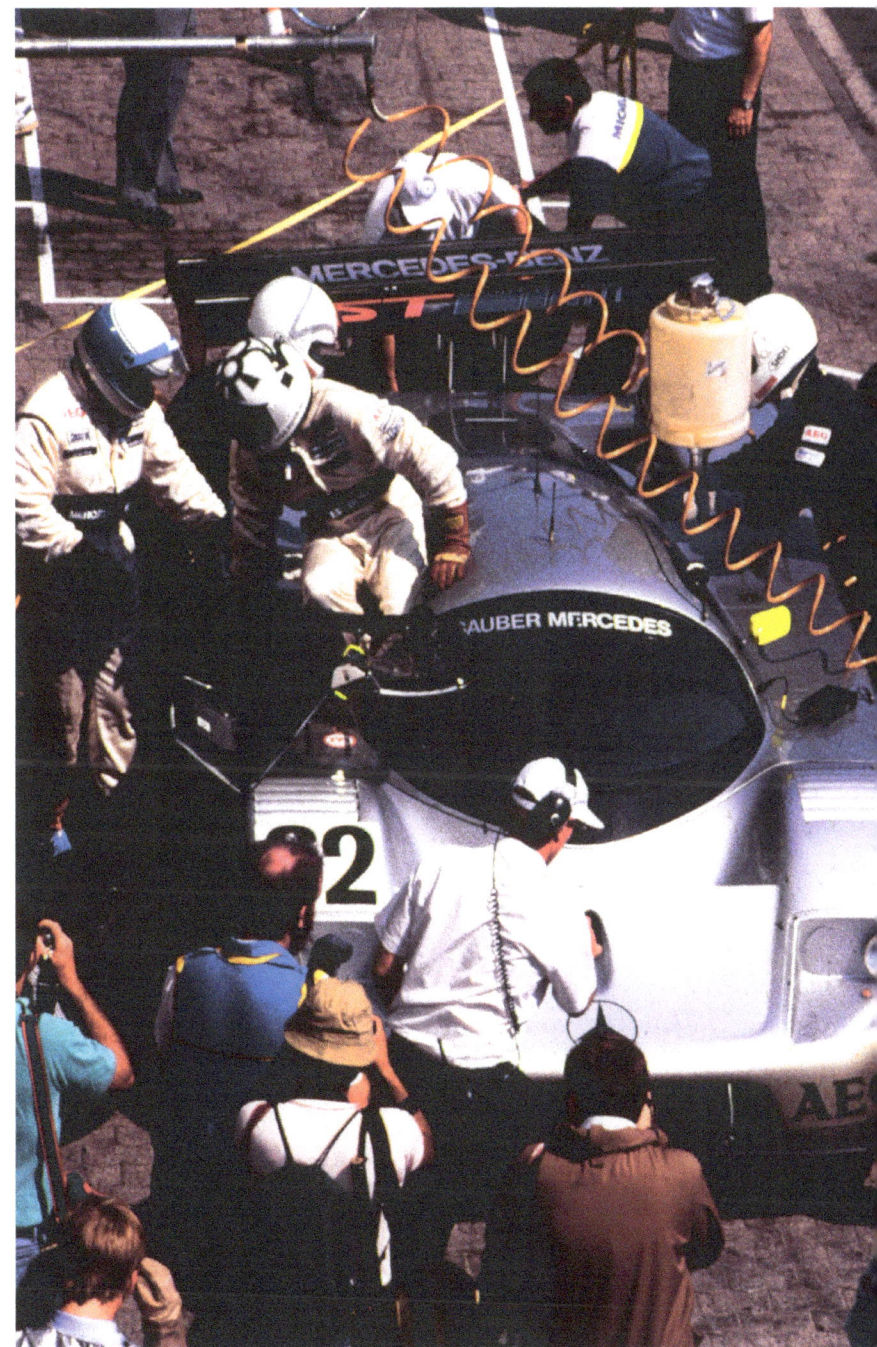

TWR-Jaguar now inherited the lead, with over a lap between him and Mauro Baldi in the leading C9. Although the Baldi/Acheson/Brancatelli Sauber-Mercedes was going well, Jochen Mass was going even better and his C9, driven now by Stanley Dickens, took over second place just before dawn. This became first place when the leading TWR-Jaguar was forced into the pits for a gearbox rebuild at 06.20 hours.

Now the Sauber-Mercedes were first and second and, despite Baldi having to replace a nose after a spin, the result looked like a Mercedes one-two victory. It almost wasn't. At a quarter to four, Kenny Acheson found that he had only fifth gear left in his car's gearbox. Nevertheless, so big was the Sauber-Mercedes lead that they crossed the line together in first, second and fifth places. The Wollek/Stuck Joest-entered Porsche filled out the top three.

Jochen Mass: "Well, when you go to do Le Mans, you never expect to win it. Too many things can go wrong! You say to yourself: 'O.K. Let's get going and see what happens.' Victory is not in your mind."

"It's so easy to lose Le Mans, by just a small thing. Manuel Reuter drove over someone's broken exhaust and the damage could have been far worse than it turned out to be in the end. The one sad thing for me, was that the race was outside the Championship. If I'd been awarded the normal points, I would have been World Champion in 1989."

Bob Bell: "Winning Le Mans with Sauber-Mercedes was one of the proudest moments in my life. I had just joined the team and done Dijon, then come to Le Mans. We did a few tiny tweaks to the cars but otherwise they were perfect. I've learned over the years that less is more in racing. You don't win Le Mans by throwing money at it, you win by having a well-developed package and team."

"The Sauber-Mercedes was a good car. A big old slug, really, but there was nothing bad in the package and that's why it was so successful. Don't forget that it had been designed by Leo Ress, quite one of the most laid-back, lovely people around."

"I remember that at a test session at Brands Hatch, Schlesser crashed chassis five in a big shunt – really bolloxed it up. The funny thing is, once that car was repaired, it went on to win the most races of all of them. Funny, really, you can't account for things like that."

Jarama, in the middle of a super-hot summer, even for central Spain, saw the spectators vote by staying away in droves. Additionally, after the effort of Le Mans, there were only twenty-four cars on the grid, the rest taking the opportunity of the one race per season exemption provided by the FISA and going for the big-monied race held at the Norisring on the same weekend.

After a struggle with the TWR-Jaguar XJR-9s, Mauro Baldi took the pole in his carbon fiber braked Sauber-Mercedes at 1:15.58 with Schlesser just a hair slower (1:15.613), and then Lammers piloted the first of the XJR-9s around at 1:16.601. The second TWR-Jaguar gridded fourth. The best Porsche 962C could only manage eleventh place (the Brun Repsol car of Oscar Larrauri and Jesus Pareja), whilst the newcomers Toyota and Nissan landed up fifth and sixth respectively.

The race turned out to be a Sauber-Mercedes benefit, the winning C9 of Schlesser and Mass lapping the second-placed XJR-9 of Lammers and Tambay. Kenny Acheson and Mauro Baldi had decided upon a more cautious strategy, taking two sessions each due to the heat. Their car led initially but brake failure sent their C9 across the gravel and then the ensuing stop had cost them three laps. Nonetheless, they had fought their way back up to fifth by the finish. The Brun Porsche had shown surprising speed (and frugality!) in the race, enabling it to finish third overall.

Perhaps the most surprising performance of all had been that of Thorkild Thyrring and Wayne Taylor in a Spice SE88 with a 3.5 DFZ Cosworth fitted. At one point, this had been up to second place. Despite a collision with Johnny Dumfries' Toyota and rooted tires, they still finished in second place!

A month later, the teams reassembled in England for the race at Brands Hatch, a superb circuit for the more nimble cars and an entry of thirty-eight saw what should have been the greatest threat to the Sauber-Mercedes take pole position.

This was the new TWR-Jaguar XJR-11 turbocharged V-6 of Jan Lammers and Patrick Tambay and it recorded a 1:12.927, as against Mauro Baldi's best of 1:13.385. Jean-Louis Schlesser was just a tad slower while the Julian Bailey/Andrew Gilbert-Scott carbon-braked Nissan R89C was just a thousandth of a second slower! The best V12 Jaguar, like the best Porsche 962 at Jarama, was back in eleventh place. The Joest entry was the Porsche 962C of Bob Wollek and Frank Jelinski, driving the car that Stuck and Wollek had driven at Le Mans (chassis number 962.145).

When the lights changed to green, the two Saubers dashed to the fore, almost having to cede to the XJR-11 of Jones/Ferte, which had grabbed third as, paradoxically, Lammers had slid straight back into fourth. The second XJR-11 was forced to stop with a damaged distributor not long after.

Schlesser and Mass then had a tire start to chunk, damaging their rear suspension, which slowed this car considerably. Happily for the German cars entered, the Jaguars suffered also, Lammers and Tambay losing a turbocharger after becoming involved in a barging match with Johnny Dumfries' Toyota, which dropped them back to fifth place at the end.

The Joest Porsche had an almost perfect race, staying out of trouble but not being able to challenge either the C9s or the Turbo Jaguars on pace. Nevertheless, they were rewarded with second at the finish. At one point, the Dumfries/Watson Toyota was up to third place, but its charge had been at the expense of fuel consumption and it ran out of fuel. Poor John Nielsen suffered a massive accident in the V-12 engined XJR-9 when his brakes failed but thankfully emerged unhurt from the debris.

After another month's gap, the circus arrived at "Der Neue" Nürburgring, a 2.8-mile track that was regarded as, at best, antiseptic by most of the drivers when compared to the old, almost fifteen-mile long circuit.

Sauber-Mercedes

In qualifying, the Sauber-Mercedes finished up occupying the front row, whilst the Jan Lammers/Patrick Tambay TWR-Jaguar was third. The Nissan R89C was next up and the Toyota and Wollek/Jelinski Joest 962C rounded out the top six places.

A disappointed Jean-Louis Schlesser stands besides his Sauber-Mercedes C9-88.05. Drawn into a pell-mell fight with Mauro Baldi and Kenny Acheson in the sister car for the Championship, Schlesser ran out of fuel one lap from victory and was not classified in the results. [Photo: Courtesy of LAT.]

WORLD CHAMPIONS – THE GROUP C CARS

Side by side at the start, the two Sauber-Mercedes C9's lead the pack in the final race of 1989 at Mexico City. Schlesser and Mass would emerge victorious, thus handing the Driver's Championship to Schlesser and the Manufacturers Championship to Sauber-Mercedes. [Photo: Courtesy of LAT.]

At the start, the two Saubers dutifully took the lead but it was not long before Andrew Gilbert-Scott's Nissan was past the pair of them and going away. Lapping some slower cars, Oscar Larrauri in the Brun Porsche 962C passed Baldi and punted

Schlesser off-course to take second place. Mass took over from Schlesser, now back in fifth place, whilst Julian Bailey was handed a comfortable lead by Andrew Gilbert-Scott.

Franz Konrad, Larrauri's co-driver, could not keep up the pace, perhaps due to fuel consumption problems, and ceded second place to Kenny Acheson, now driving the Sauber-Mercedes that he shared with Mauro Baldi. The TWR-Jaguars were well off the pace at this time, the best being in tenth place.

Jochen Mass was up to third place and, in the ensuing pitstop, his co-driver, Jean-Louis Schlesser, got out ahead of the sister car. Still ahead of Schlesser was the fleeing Nissan, but Julian Bailey was forced to slack off his pace, due to the fuel consumption being too high to see him through to the finish. In the event, he ran out of fuel and was not classified, but the Nissan's performance had still shaken the Germans.

By now, Bob Wollek had forced his way through the entire field and was in front in the Joest Porsche 962C. The last ten laps saw a great scrap between the two German cars with Schlesser just coming out on top when Wollek's 962C also ran out of fuel on the next to last lap. Baldi made it a Sauber-Mercedes one-two but it had been a worrying home ground race.

Donington in England was next and the C9's were again on the front row and once again made it a one-two. However, that was not the whole story of this race.

The Lola-Nissan of Julian Bailey/Mark Blundell was third on the grid with the Toyota fourth. The TWR Turbo Jaguars were on the third row of the grid.

For once, Jan Lammers made a good start and got by both the Nissan and Toyota in front of him and set off after Schlesser, whom he also soon passed. Baldi in the other C9 had a good start and was off like a rabbit with Lammers in hot pursuit. The Toyota clouted a curb and was never in contention, and the Nissan was also catching Schlesser and shortly thereafter, got by.

Lammers' Jaguar passed Baldi's C9 when he missed a shift but his lead did not last long as Schlesser now slipstreamed his team mate and used the momentum to pass not only him, but Lammers too! For the next few laps, the Sauber-Mercedes and the Jaguar traded places with Baldi third and the Nissan fourth. Wayne Taylor in the Spice now entered the fight, overtaking both Bailey in the Nissan and Lammers. Sadly, the Spice went out with electrical problems shortly after this. Tambay also fell out when the Jaguar's distributor drive broke again.

After pit stops, the Nissan emerged with a ten-second lead, but was penalized for having the fuel flow too quickly through the refueling rig. Mark Blundell took over and proceeded to fend off the C9s. He led from laps thirty-seven to eighty-nine, until having to pit for the crew's infraction, at

Champion at last! Moments after the end of the race at Mexico City, Jean-Louis Schlesser is exultant whilst Max Welti congratulates him. [Photo: Courtesy of LAT.]

which point, Schlesser took over at the front.

The final part of the race saw Baldi's C9, Bailey's Nissan and Wollek's Porsche all fighting for second place, a struggle from which Baldi emerged victorious, the Nissan cruising home with a worn-out tire in third and Wollek having to settle for fourth place.

Thus it was that Sauber-Mercedes finished first and second and that Mercedes had won the Sports-Prototype World Championship, a Championship that Mercedes had last won in 1955.

With the Championship for Makes already won, there was only the struggle for the drivers' crown to be fought for now. Only a Sauber-Mercedes driver could win this and Schlesser had a few more points in hand than Mauro Baldi when the field next assembled at the very fast and daunting circuit at Spa-Francorchamps, the home of the Belgian Grand Prix.

The usual Ardennes weather saw qualifying become a lottery. Schlesser and Mass fought a misfire and wheelbearing problems to take a lowly (for them!) sixth place on the grid. The Lola-Nissan, using its by now usual mix of bias-ply front and radial rear tires, must have been a real handful here and seventh place in qualifying reflected this.

Mauro Baldi, however, had no problems and set pole in 2:05.90. Jan Lammers' XJR-11 took the outside of the front row in 2:07.84 with John Nielsen third in the second XJR-11. Bob Wollek put Joest's 962C on the outside of the second row, and the Dumfries/Geoff Lees Toyota was fifth.

The start, from the F1 grid situated between the Bus stop chicane and the La Source hairpin, was chaotic. Effectively only wide enough for one car, La Source saw three abreast as Lammers and the two Sauber-Mercedes C9s hurtled around it. From La Source down to Eau Rouge is flat out and the C9s demonstrated their power advantage over the Jaguar and pulled away into a one-two lead. Baldi led with Schlesser following and behind Lammers, Julian Bailey's Nissan had grabbed fourth.

Behind them was chaos as two Porsches and one Toyota attempted to follow, Dumfries having his nose damaged as Wollek chopped him off. The Nissan backed off to conserve fuel and let the Toyota and Larrauri's Brun-entered 962C pass by.

Both Jaguars were out by lap twenty-six, Lammers being the first to retire when a turbo's oil seals let go. The other Jaguar lost its electrics due to a wiring problem. Mauro Baldi, partnered by Kenny Acheson, never looked like losing their lead and Bob Wollek and Frank Jelinski took second when the second Sauber-Mercedes ran out of fuel at the end of the race.

Dave Price: "With Mercedes backing, we were expected to win every race, not only that, but to come in one-two, if possible. We were devastated if we lost a race. I remember Schlesser's engine coughing on the last lap at Spa as he came out of the bus-stop chicane and ran out of fuel. There was hell to pay for that."

The Lola-Nissan's "cruise" mode proved to be the best of the rest with Bailey and Blundell placing third. Larrauri and Ratzenberger were fourth in their Brun 962C, belaying the fact that the Porsche was, at this stage, an eight-year-old design!

And so to the last round of 1989, held in Mexico City. To win the Driver's Championship, Mauro Baldi had to win outright. He started in great form, putting the C9 on the pole again, almost a second faster than Schlesser's sister car. The Johnny Dumfries/John Watson Toyota was next up with the Wollek/Jelinski Joest Porsche 962C in fourth. Lammers and Tambay could only manage fifth place on this power circuit and Oscar Larrauri and Harald Huysman took the sixth spot in their Brun-entered 962C. The Lola-Nissan could do no better than eighth.

Jean-Louis Schlesser had no intention of ceding the title to his Italian team-mate and took the lead immediately, pulling out a second and a half per lap. The Toyota, Nissan and Larrauri's Porsche tried to catch up, but were relegated to also-ran status by the C9s. Poor Wollek was disqualified when the Joest crew attempted to push-start the Porsche after it refused to start on the grid.

As Baldi pitted for new tires and fuel, Bruno Giacomelli's Lancia LC2 lost its rear wing and crashed, bringing out the pace car. Schlesser passed the pace car but Baldi did not, putting his Sauber-Mercedes a lap down on the leading car. Fortunately, the pace car waved the following cars by and when the race re-commenced, Baldi was up with Schlesser, but Schlesser once more pulled away. Baldi handed over to Kenny Acheson who tried hard but overdid it and crashed the Sauber-Mercedes.

Kenny Acheson: "I was lucky to race with Mercedes-Benz in 1989. They were a very friendly team, lovely people. They made the right decision in hiring Schumacher, Frentzen and Wendlinger for 1990. I got to know both Karl and Heinz-Harald later on, lovely people."

Oscar Larrauri, Harald Huysman, Henri Pescarolo and Frank Jelinski took a superb second and third for the Brun 962Cs and Derek Bell and Tiff Needell gave the Richard Lloyd-entered Porsche 962C it's best result of the season in fourth place. The two XJR-9s of Tom Walkinshaw Racing salvaged some honor for a dismal season, finishing fifth and sixth.

But at Mercedes and Sauber, all was joy. Not only had one of their drivers won the Driver's Championship, they had also claimed the Manufacturer's crown, less than two years after Mercedes declared their backing of Peter Sauber's team.

That the Sauber-Mercedes C9 was better than the other, competing Group C cars could not be doubted. In terms of speed, handling, fuel efficiency and driver comfort, there was little doubt amongst the competition of who had the best car that season.

However, there were warning signs. The TWR Jaguars were always in the hunt and Reinhold Joest was having success with his much-modified Porsche 962C. Also, Nissan had burst onto the scene with an excellent car, (even though, to all intents and purposes, it was a Lola). Add to this that the lightweight Spices were becoming ever more threatening and Sauber could see that another, better car was needed. Leo Ress set to work in late 1989 to produce probably the greatest of the Swiss-German line, the C11.

Chapter 6

Mercedes Developments 1989-1990

Sauber-Mercedes

Over the close season of 1989-1990, Mercedes made several important changes to the team that had proved to be so dominant in 1989. The management wanted to stamp Mercedes' superiority over any of its competitors, much in the way that it had done in the thirties with the "Silver Arrows" Grand Prix team. Adopting the solo name, "Mercedes" instead of the previous "Sauber-Mercedes", was just a first step. Apart from the silver paint scheme and the three-pointed star on the front of the cars, "Mercedes" was now shown in large letters across the top of their windshields.

To accomplish this mastery, Mercedes advanced not only on a technical front with improvements to the cars themselves, but they also changed their driver line up. Out went the talented Kenny Acheson and in came three young drivers, Austrian Karl Wendlinger (the then-current German F3 Champion) and Germans Heinz-Harald Frentzen and a certain Michael Schumacher, whom the World would shortly hear a lot more of when he moved into Formula One. Jochen Mass was given the job of tutoring these three "apprentices" in the job of driving the new Mercedes C11, whilst Mauro Baldi was now paired with Jean-Louis Schlesser in the other team car. The new team members covered thousands of miles of testing the C9 and the C11 during the winter months.

Jochen Neerpasch was now in charge of the racing effort and the Sauber team took their orders from him.

The new Mercedes C11 was an evolution of the Sauber-Mercedes C9, again designed by Leo Ress. The first chassis was built in Switzerland, but this was not a success, proving to be too heavy as the Swiss lacked experience in building carbon composites and so the building of this new chassis was contracted out to Dave Price's company, DPS (David Price-Philip Sharp) Composites in Surrey, England. This was almost ironic, in light of the fact that Dave Price, having managed the Mercedes squad during 1989 was then headhunted by Nissan, to run their Group C team in 1990. Price promptly hired Kenny Acheson to drive the Lola-Nissan R90C. Frank Coppuck set up a

Previous Page: Now proudly wearing the number 1 to denote the car of the World Champion, Jean-Louis Schlesser in the new Mercedes C11 makes a dramatic picture. [Photo: Courtesy of Daimler/Chrysler Archives.]

The Mercedes C11. Gone now was the Sauber name, although the cars were designed at Sauber's headquarters. This is the car driven at Le Mans by Jean-Louis Schlesser, Jochen Mass and Alain Ferte. The engine failed with less than two hours to run. [Photo: Courtesy of Daimler/Chrysler Archives.]

four-man team in Hinwil, where Coppuck designed and made the moulds for the carbon fiber over honeycomb aluminum chassis.

The C11 was said to have twice the torsional stiffness of the older C9 aluminum monocoque and this made the choice of springing and damping critical. Leo Ress:

The C11 at Le Mans in 1991. This one was driven by Jonathan Palmer, Kurt Thiim and Stanley Dickens but retired after fifteen hours running. Despite being a new design, the C11 had few problems, steamrollering the opposition by winning eight out of nine races counting towards the World Sportscar Championship in 1990. [Photo: Courtesy of Daimler/Chrysler Archives.]

"Really, the C11 was just a modification of the C9 – nothing unknown. Of course, the C11 had the composite chassis and we had to be more precise in the way that we set up the car, but a stiffer chassis definitely allowed us more in the way of advantage."

"We designed the C11 with a longer wheelbase for greater stability, and this time, we used a wind tunnel with a rolling road, as they do in Formula One. The new pushrod suspension design also made it much easier to set up the car for any given track."

Ress narrowed the windshield and cockpit of the C11, when compared to that of the C9. Apart from two vertical slots to funnel cool air to the driver in the nose, the majority of the C11's bodywork looked almost identical to that of the C9s.

Where there was a difference was in the underbody. The new venturi started from further forward than had the C9s, thus being more efficient. This gave a marked improvement in downforce without increasing drag. The weight distribution was pushed further forward with an increase in the wheelbase from 106.25 to 109 inches. This decreased the curse of Group C/GTP cars: a lack of front end grip that usually resulted in marked understeer.

The biggest single difference between the C9 and the C11 was in the suspension. This was now of the pushrod variety, closely following the swing to this in Formula One. At the rear, the coil-spring damper units were placed transversely above the differential, operated through rocker arms. This system allowed the team to adjust the wheel-rebound extension without changing ride height, which, in a ground-effect car, is critical.

The C11 featured a new and stronger gearbox, Bosch 1.8 engine management and further improvements to the already fuel-efficient and powerful M119 engine. Amongst these further improvements were smaller diameter camshafts, still built with the 'assembly' method peculiar to this engine. There were also new magnesium camshaft covers, and the use of titanium was increased to include the flywheel and crankshaft damper.

The turbochargers came in for this type of development also. The compressor's turbine wheel was now made in magnesium and, at the last race of the season in Mexico City, wheels made of ceramic material were used. In this way, forty percent of the turbocharger's rotating mass was decreased, and this reduced the response time needed to build pressure in the plenum chamber from one to just half a second. Rotating inertia was thus reduced and responsiveness to the driver's right foot increased.

Narrower piston rings reduced friction losses, and even the skirts of the cup followers in the valve train were drilled to lighten them. Most engines now used a single-row timing chain, but for Le Mans the old double version was used to aid reliability over the twenty-four hours.

Down to Redgate Corner at Donington comes the Schlesser/Baldi Mercedes C11.03 in 1990, a race that the pairing duly won. [Photo: Courtesy of LAT.]

The engine's actual weight did not vary much from the year before, as the dry-sump assembly was now made in aluminum, instead of the previously-used magnesium. This was thought to be too weak for the job (although it had proved reliable enough in 1989) but, more importantly, all this work lowered the engine's center of gravity.

The new Bosch Motronic MP 1.8 engine management system featured individual ignition timing for each cylinder. Not only this, the system was of the self-learning type. Individual cylinders now had their own, detonation-sensing coil whose sensor was embedded in the combustion chamber's roof. The advantage of this system lay in the fact that the maximum period of ignition advance could now be used in each cylinder on every firing stroke, detonation being sensed and the timing retarded as necessary. This Bosch MP 1.8 system required a dedicated wiring loom and a data-acquisition system that included telemetry. The increased fuel efficiency of the M119 engine in its 1990 form allowed the team to tune the chassis for increased downforce in race trim as consumption during a race was no longer critical.

The new gearbox of the C11 had a bulkhead that gave extra support between first and second gears. Only one sideplate (to allow access to the differential) was designed into the case that held first and reverse gear, the ring and pinion, and the bellhousing between the engine and the new gearbox. Behind this was the magnesium case that held the easily changeable top four gear pairs. The internal components were the same as those of the Hewland VGC gearbox, enabling X-Trak and Staffs silent gears to provide parts. The previously-used Michelin tires gave way to Goodyears. The combination of new suspension design and the transition to Goodyear tires markedly improved traction, particularly at the rear. So stiff was the basic rear suspension design that a rear anti-roll bar was hardly ever needed.

Peter Sauber talking with Max Welti, ex-driver and the Sauber Team Manager. [Photo: Courtesy of LAT.]

CHAPTER 7

Mercedes Racing in 1990

The Group C Formula, as the rules had been framed, was slated to come to an end in 1990. A new formula for 3.5-liter atmospheric engined lightweight cars without a restricted fuel allocation was due to come into effect in 1991. To develop a car for just one season was a very expensive way to do things but it shows the level of commitment that Mercedes applied to winning.

Group C/Sports car racing in Europe, in marked contrast to the successful IMSA-run GTP series in America, was in a parlous state in 1991. Spectator attendance (except for Le Mans) dwindled to the point that, at Spa Francorchamps, there were probably more team personnel than there were paying public.

Most of this was the fault of the organizing body, the FIA. They had demanded television rights from the Automobile Club d'Ouest, which the organizers of the Le Mans 24-Hour race were unwilling to hand over, rightly reasoning that they were more important to sports car racing than all the other races put together. In response, the FIA excluded the race from the Championship. It made no difference to the race's attendance, but it severely hurt the other races. During this period, the FIA was attempting to make sports car racing a twin to its successful Formula One series. The governing body simply misunderstood that sports car fans were not into sprint format races and liked big, powerful two-seaters instead of the quasi-F1 cars that the FIA were determined to introduce.

Jochen Mass: "The moment I heard that Bernie Ecclestone had taken over the promotion of the Group C Championship, I knew that it was doomed. I thought: 'Why would Bernie be interested in doing this'?"

"Mercedes offered me the chance to coach the youngsters and I thought: 'There goes my chance of becoming World Champion in Sportscars.' It took me about an hour of thinking about it before I said 'Yes, o.k. – let's do it.' I knew my time in World-class racing was coming to an end and this seemed to be a good way to leave the sport."

The Le Mans-less Championship kicked off at Suzuka and, like 1989, was a 480 kms sprint race. As in 1989, it also resulted in a Mercedes one-two.

The first C11 chassis was used for qualifying, but Jean-Louis Schlesser crashed it on Saturday, damaging it enough for the team to decide to put it away in the trailer and use the two C9/89s that they had brought for the race itself.

Unusually, Mercedes were not on pole position, which had been taken in a Banzai qualifying lap by Geoff Lees in a TOMS Toyota 90CV. Roland Ratzenberger took third on the grid in another Toyota 90CV. The first Mercedes was that of Schlesser and Baldi in second place with Mass and Wendlinger occupying the fourth slot. Hoshino was fifth in a Nissan R89C and Dumfries and Suzuki rounded out the top six with yet another Toyota. The TWR Jaguars occupied seventh and eighth starting slots and were more competitive than these positions suggested, but preferred to concentrate on race, rather than qualifying set-ups.

Schlesser and Baldi celebrate on the podium after their victory at Suzuka whilst Jochen Mass looks on. The third placed Nissan crew of Masahiro Hasemi and Anders Olofsson wait their turn to spray the champagne. [Photo: Courtesy of LAT.]

Sweeping through the Ascari chicane ahead of a Porsche 962C goes the Schlesser/Baldi Mercedes C11 on its way to victory. [Photo: Courtesy of LAT.]

Jochen Mass: "The C11 was a big improvement over the C9. Dave Price did sterling work on it, and so did Leo (Ress). The stiffer chassis helped to make the car less physical to drive than the C9 had been."

Jean-Louis Schlesser had to start from the pit lane after his car's fuel tank sprang a leak and Mass spun on the first lap, allowing the TWR Jaguar XJR-11 of Brundle and Alain Ferte to lead through to the middle of the race, so improved were they over the 1989 versions. Both Jaguars were then put out through engine failure.

Karl Wendlinger overtook Alain Ferte but had to give best to the number one Mercedes of Schlesser and Baldi and then,

Norbert Haug, the Mercedes representative (on left of picture), looks on from the pits at Silverstone where the Mercedes team suffered their only defeat of the season – by Jaguar. [Photo: Courtesy of LAT.]

when the other Jaguar's engine failed, the Mercedes cruised home as the remaining contenders throttled back to preserve their dwindling fuel supply. Hasemi and Olofsson finished third in the Lola-Nissan R90C after having been involved in the first lap Mercedes spin. Porsche had switched from Goodyear tires to Michelins and suffered for it, the 962 not being as suited to the stronger Goodyears as the C11. The best 962 finish was that of Takahashi and Mogi in fifth place.

To Europe next, where the season started in Italy at Monza. Mauro Baldi qualified the number one Mercedes on pole position at 1:29.165, an average speed of almost 139 mph. Baldi used the new second C11 car to be built, Mass and Karl Wendlinger sharing C11-01. They posted second fastest at 1:30.113. The team had also brought along the last C9 (chassis number C9-88.06) as a spare. It wasn't needed.

The two XJR-11 Jaguars now occupied the second row and it looked as if a hard fight might be a prospect, the other teams hoping that the new C11 might encounter problems, but they had not reckoned on Mercedes' thoroughness in winter testing.

For the rest of the grid, NME (Nissan Motorsport Europe) had entered two of their new Lola-Nissan R90Cs. Mark Blundell placed one of these fourth in qualifying. The Joest-entered 962C of Jonathan Palmer and Tiff Needell was fifth, a Toyota 90CV was sixth and Julian Bailey qualified the second Nissan in seventh place. His co-driver was Kenny Acheson.

At the start, Mauro Baldi shot off to a lead that was never to be relinquished, while Mass spun yet again at the first corner, this time taking Jan Lammers off with him. Mass and Wendlinger fought back and, on the last lap, Mass overtook the second placed Jaguar, whose fuel was running out. In fact, Brundle ran out completely on the cool-off lap whilst the Mercedes had fuel to spare. Wollek and Jelinski in Joest's 962C managed fifth place, on the same lap as the fourth placed Jaguar but the rest were lapped at least twice.

Then came the British Empire Trophy at Silverstone, where the British fans were yearning for revenge after the Jaguar's defeat of the year before. Amazingly, they got it.

In practice, Michael Schumacher, partnering Jochen Mass, stopped at Copse Corner, near the end of the pit exit with a broken gear linkage. The Mercedes mechanics went to help him, which was against the rules and the second Mercedes was disqualified from the race. Despite this setback, Schlesser still put the "lead" Mercedes on pole position. Brundle and Lammers qualified the two Jaguar XJR-11s in second and third places, but Brundle was almost a second slower than Schlesser, an ominous omen for the race.

WORLD CHAMPIONS – THE GROUP C CARS

Following Silverstone came Spa-Francorchamps, the great circuit set in the Ardennes, and once again, the Mercedes C11 re-asserted its superiority, Jochen Mass and Karl Wendlinger beating the Jaguar XJR-11 of Jan Lammers and Andy Wallace. [Photo: Courtesy of LAT.]

Blundell's Nissan took fourth place and the Richard Lloyd-entered Porsche 962 driven by Jonathan Palmer was fifth. Geoff Lees' Toyota filled the sixth slot on the start line grid.

Schlesser and Baldi led comfortably during the race to build a forty-eight second lead, but then Mercedes suffered their first engine failure in the series. The timing chain had broken. This left the two XJR-11

Jaguars to take first and second places, despite having to scrap with the Nissans, both of whom ran short of fuel at the end. The third placed Spice SE90C of Velez and Giacomelli was the only other car to finish on the same lap as the second placed Jaguar, no one else being near the top finishers.

Spa-Francorchamps in Belgium next, in June, and Mauro Baldi set a qualifying pace that neither Jaguar could

Seen rounding the La Source hairpin at Spa, the winning C11 displays its beautiful lines. [Photo: Courtesy of LAT.]

get near. Baldi qualified his C11 in 1:59.35, an average speed of over 130 mph. The first Jaguar, that of Brundle, was three seconds slower than Baldi. Jochen Mass was second, joined again in the cockpit by Karl Wendlinger. The timing of the race, by the FIA, was a blatant attempt to interfere with the entry at Le Mans, so close were the dates. All this succeeded in doing was to upset the teams.

Although practice and qualifying had taken place in dry weather, light rain greeted the competitors as they made their way around the pace lap. After just a few laps, a dry line appeared and most competitors charged into the pits for a change to slicks. The exceptions were the two leading Mercedes who stayed out on their fast deteriorating wets. Martin Brundle made the most of it to catch and pass the leading C11. The Mercedes were trying to stay out till their scheduled pit stops and make one less stop than everyone else. They almost didn't make it, Jochen Mass' car keeping to the plan but the Baldi/Schlesser C11 needed seven minutes in the pits to fix an ignition problem, putting it out of contention for a top six finish. Brundle's Jaguar was now in a very good position, Mass' Mercedes having to ease back to conserve its fuel supply. Sadly for Jaguar, a second consecutive win was not to be as the XJR-11 caught fire.

At the flag, the Mercedes was ninety seconds ahead of the Jaguar of Jan Lammers and Andy Wallace whilst the Lola-Nissan R90C at last took a podium finish. These three cars were the only ones to complete the entire seventy laps of the race.

Mercedes boycotted the 1990 Le Mans 24-Hours in the hopes that this would force the A.C. de l'Ouest and the FIA to come to an agreement, but that didn't happen and they were missed. This year saw a tremendous entry and a great race, won by TWR-Jaguar with their now venerable XJR-12s. No less than seven Nissans were entered, Blundell's setting a qualifying time that has yet to be beaten, as this book went to press. What could Mercedes have done? We shall never know.

On then, to Dijon – Prenois and Schlesser took pole position, something the other teams had been forced to get used to. Mass, this time partnered by Michael Schumacher, made it a Mercedes one-two on the grid, the Jaguars placing third and fourth.

The race proper had to be restarted after a first-lap shunt that saw only the two Mercedes and Jaguars get away cleanly. At the re-start, the Mercedes again stormed ahead but this time, it was Julian Bailey in the Lola-Nissan who gave chase to the fleeing C11s. The Jaguars followed on. Dumfries' Jaguar chose this moment to blow its engine and Lammers, right behind him slid off the track, as did Kenny Acheson in the second Nissan.

The Mercedes C11s drew out a second a lap lead to take the victory, with

Nürburgring. The winning C11 of Schlesser and Baldi. [Photo: Courtesy of LAT.]

the Nissan third (again!) and Jan Lammers and Andy Wallace bringing the delayed TWR-Jaguar XJR-11 home in fourth place. Martin Brundle and Alain Ferte took fifth, with the Spice SE90 of Wayne Taylor and Eliseo Salazar sixth.

By now, Mercedes had a commanding lead in the Championship, the TWR-Jaguar, Nissans and Toyotas being unable, it seemed, to take the fight to the C11's, no matter how hard they tried. The Porsche 962Cs were now outclassed,

Michael Schumacher driving the Mercedes C11 that he and Jochen Mass drove to second place at the Nürburgring. [Photo: Courtesy of LAT.]

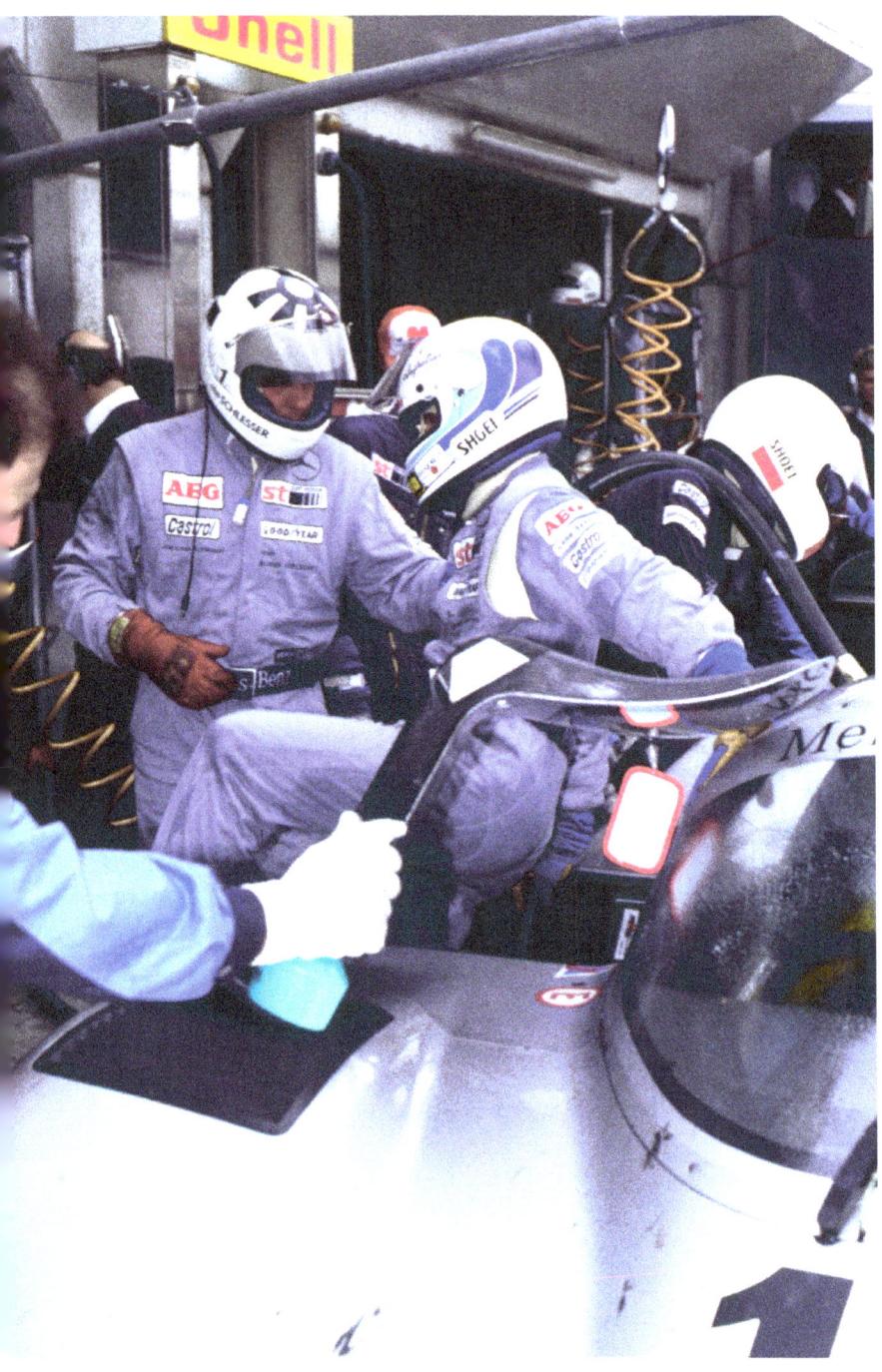

Mauro Baldi climbs out as Jean-Louis Schlesser prepares to take his place in the winning C11 during a pitstop in the Nürburgring race. [Photo: Courtesy of LAT.]

although the switch to Michelin rubber was the main cause of this, the venerable chassis design simply refusing to lie down and die.

At the Nürburgring, it was another Mercedes one-two, business as usual, the two Mercedes lapping the entire field up to third place.

Donington on September 2nd was notable for Mercedes, giving Heinz-Harald Frentzen his first race in one of the Silver Arrows. He was co-driving with Jochen Mass.

Donington is hard on tires and brakes, and Julian Bailey's Nissan led Jochen Mass at the start. Bailey had to slow to conserve fuel and Mass was soon past him: the Mercedes fuel frugality by now the class of the field. Tim Harvey, in his Spice, also got past Bailey.

At the first stops, Martin Brundle got out ahead of Frentzen, and the crowd was treated to a thrilling dice as the Jaguar and Mercedes swapped second place several times. Ahead of them, untroubled, was the Schlesser/Baldi C11, stretching out its lead in front of the scrapping pair behind it.

Frentzen finally got the Mercedes into an untroubled second place as Brundle slacked off to conserve fuel and the C11 pair drove to another one-two, despite the leading car stopping for a quick inspection when leaking oil dropped onto the exhaust and caused a worrying smoke trail.

Sadly for TWR, Brundle's Jaguar was later excluded from the results when it was found that both XJR-11s had taken on too much fuel. This elevated the Spice into third place and the Acheson/Brancatelli Lola-Nissan up to fourth.

The combined points won by the Mercedes team at the Donington race made them Champions again with two races still to go.

These two races were held on the American continent, the first being in Canada, at Mosport. and it was notable for two things, the first being the appearance of the Matra-designed Peugeot 905, France's V-10 3.5-liter "Atmo" contender. Keke Rosberg had been persuaded out of retirement to drive and the car looked, sounded and went well.

In qualifying, it was the same old story except that whilst Jean-Louis Schlesser took pole position, the second C11, driven by Mass and Wendlinger, was in fourth place at the start, Mark Blundell in the Lola-Nissan in second and Martin Brundle placed the TWR-Jaguar in third place.

Although Schlesser led briefly at the start, Martin Brundle demoted the Frenchman to second in short order. The Jaguar led until lap twenty-eight when it stopped for fuel. Schlesser was in one lap later but Mauro Baldi came out in eighth place. After a second yellow flag period, Bailey in the Lola-Nissan led until Mauro Baldi caught and passed him on lap fifty-nine.

It was at this time that the second notable occurrence at the Montreal race took place. The manhole covers on this street circuit had not been welded down properly and first of all Henri Moran's Cougar was damaged severely when one was dislodged. This was rapidly followed by Jesus Pareja's Brun-entered 962C being hit in the windshield by flying debris as a manhole cover sliced open the monocoque and allowed fuel to reach the hot engine, causing the Porsche to erupt into a fireball as Pareja slid into the guardrails. Luckily, Pareja emerged with little more than shock and minor burns, as did Harold Huysman, whose 962C, right behind Pareja, had also hit the wall in the confusion.

The race was stopped on lap sixty-one and half-points awarded to Schlesser and Baldi. Sadly for poor Mass, Wendlinger had pitted the lap before the accident and was thus demoted in the final results.

SAUBER-MERCEDES

It was all Schlesser needed to claim the Drivers' Championship, but no one (least of all the Mercedes drivers) was happy to see the Championship won in such a way.

For the final race of the season, held at Mexico City, TWR-Jaguar took pole position, Martin Brundle doing a 1:20.62. Surprisingly, neither Schlesser nor Baldi was next, second going to Jochen Mass, the sister car taking third. Geoff Lees put the Toyota in fourth place with Bailey's Nissan next up, followed

A depressingly normal sight for the opposition in 1990. Mercedes first and second, Jaguar third. On the podium are Jean Louis Schlesser and Mauro Baldi (winners) and Michael Schumacher and Jochen Mass (second place). Not pictured, Martin Brundle and Alain Ferte (Jaguar XJR-11) were third. [Photo: Courtesy of LAT.]

The view that most of the opposition saw of a Mercedes C11 Silver Arrow in 1990. [Photo: Courtesy of LAT.]

by the Andy Wallace/Davy Jones driven XJR-11.

Brundle led at the start and resisted Jochen Mass' attempts to pass for several laps. Just as Mauro Baldi's C11 hove into view of the first two, Mass managed to out-brake Brundle and took the lead. A few more laps and Baldi was through into second place and Julian Bailey's Lola-Nissan was now threatening the Jaguar. Brundle got his second wind and took back second place from Baldi but Baldi responded and Brundle's XJR-11 spun as Baldi slipped down the inside of it. Brundle pitted for fresh rubber but electrical problems intervened, resulting in the Jaguar's eventual retirement. A faulty alternator was blamed.

At the first regular stops, Julian Bailey's Nissan took on less fuel than the two C11's and Mark Blundell, his co-driver, came out in first place. Schumacher was now driving the second C11 and, when Schlesser's Mercedes developed a vibration, overtook both him and Blundell to take the lead. Schlesser also passed Blundell, who stopped for more fuel.

Michael Schumacher brought the C11 in for Mass, who was able to come out in the lead, thanks to Schumacher's speed in the middle stint. Kenny Acheson: "I was driving the R90C and it was not slow, but on the bumpy back-straight at Mexico City, Schumacher just came flying by, leaping from bump to bump. I guess that was where I realized that he was something special."

With the end in sight, a sudden rainstorm sent cars spinning everywhere. Mauro Baldi pitted for wets immediately – the correct choice, as it turned out – resulting in victory for Baldi as his C11 was the first to take the checkered flag.

However, at post-race scrutineering, it was found that the Schlesser/Baldi C11 had taken on a tenth of a liter of fuel too much, and so it was disqualified, the Mass/Schumacher Mercedes taking the win. Not a satisfactory way for either the race, or season to end. Still, it was the end of the fuel-restricted formula, or so everyone thought.

CHAPTER 8

Fresh Start – The C291

1991 was the year that the 3.5-liter, naturally aspirated, fuel-free formula was due to take over the Championship. That it did not work out that way was due to the fact that there simply weren't enough contenders or sponsors interested in what were basically F1 cars with Sports-prototype-style bodies on them.

A combination of factors, not least the cost of building and maintaining such expensive pieces of machinery, were responsible for this state of affairs. Add in the FIA/FISA squabble with Le Mans, plus a worldwide economy that was on the slide into recession, and the outlook was bleak for sportscar racing as 1991 loomed.

The FIA, therefore, decreed that the so-called category two turbo cars (the 'old' large capacity-engined cars) could run again in 1991, having their minimum weight ballasted to 1000 kilograms (2200 pounds), and having a fuel allocation of 51-liters of fuel per 100 kilometers of distance run. As this worked out to roughly 5 mpg, it was still an attainable goal for a racing sports car. Accordingly, the decision was taken at Mercedes and Sauber to run ballasted C11s at the beginning of the season.

The new C291 was another Leo Ress design, again with a composite chassis built by DPS in Britain. Daimler-Benz had made the decision to build a 3.5-liter engine for the C291 in 1988, and fourteen different configurations were considered by design staff, including ten and twelve cylinder designs. The decision was finally taken to build a flat-12, this being seen as offering the lowest possible center of gravity, combined with the cleanest underbody aerodynamics. A single, full-width under-car venturi was considered the most effective aerodynamically.

The drive from this flat-12, as on Porsche's 917 from over twenty years before, was taken from the middle of the crankshaft, thus raising the center of gravity but, finally, a good compromise was reached after the gearbox had been redesigned.

Engine-wise, the new unit now used a TAG Electronics management system. The design department had aimed at realizing 650 bhp from the twelve-cylinder engine, but it is not known if this

---

Previous page: The new 1991 Mercedes C291 was a radical departure from the previous designs, featuring a normally-aspirated flat twelve-cylinder engine of 3.5-liters, compared with the turbocharged V8 5-litre engine previously used. Despite teething problems, the C291 was a successful design. Behind this example is a Peugeot 905, the car that gave Mercedes the toughest battles in 1991-2. [Photo: Courtesy of Daimler-Chrysler Archives.]

The Jochen Mass/Heinz-Harald Frentzen C291 at Autopolis, Mexico. [Photo: Courtesy of LAT.]

was attained in practice. Leo Ress had intended that an engine change should take no longer than three hours but, in practice, it could take up to eight hours, leaving Sauber-Mercedes mechanics looking very worried when their C291s went out for the race morning warm-up.

Leo Ress: "The C291 was philosophically different to the C9 and the C11. For a start, although the chassis was similar in design to the C11s, it had a carbon fiber/titanium rollbar structure bonded into the chassis itself. I designed pull-rod suspension for the new car, as the bodywork of the C291 was tighter and more confining than either the C9 or the C11."

"Mercedes had not built a full race engine from scratch like the flat-12 of the C291 since the fifties and they suffered from a lack of experience. This showed in the details, which complicated production. I think, when we first started, the engine would rev. to 12,000 rpm but after just one season, it went to 14,000 rpm."

"We built four or five C291s and, for the next season, we lightened the car still further, changed the bodywork and designed this new car as the C293. We made two of those. They are at the Sauber factory at Hinwil. They never even turned a single lap. Such a pity."

The new C291 was first of all entrusted to Michael Schumacher and Karl Wendlinger to drive, with Schlesser and Mass allotted the older, ballasted C11 with which to start the season.

The opposition was stiffer this year. Not only had TWR an extremely effective challenger, in the shape of the new, March-built XJR-14, with its re-badged Cosworth HB F1 3.5-liter engine (now driven by Martin Brundle, Mark Blundell, Teo Fabi and Derek Warwick) but there was also the developed Peugeot 905 "Evo" to be concerned about. Peugeot had hired a top line driving squad, including Mauro Baldi, the aforementioned Keke Rosberg, Philippe Alliot and Yannick Dalmas. Toyota and Mazda both also supplied 3.5-liter opposition, Mazda with the four-rotor 787B whilst Spice, although now out of business, had built up a lightweight 3.5 atmo car, that had shown well in 1990.

CHAPTER 9

1991 – The Final Season

At Suzuka in April, only fifteen cars started the race and only six of these were the new order 3.5-liter "F1" cars, making the allocation of the first ten grid slots for these cars a farce. However, the new cars showed a turn of speed that confounded many observers, Derek Warwick in the XJR-14 setting the pole position time of 1:48.04, some 2.5 seconds faster than Keke Rosberg could manage with the Peugeot 905.

Almost embarrassingly, the new C291 Sauber-Mercedes (Sauber's name had now re-appeared in the entry list) in the hands of the young hot-shoes, Schumacher and Wendlinger, proved to be slower than the old, ballasted, C11. Both Schlesser and Mass complained that the extra ballast in their C11 made the steering very twitchy.

In the race itself, the new TWR-Jaguar XJR-14s simply streaked away at the start but the most surprising thing was that Jean-Louis Schlesser's C11 proved to be slower than Manuel Reuter's Kremer built and entered Porsche 962C. Brundle's Jaguar stopped out on the circuit when water from his drinks bottle found its way into the electrics. The C291, Wendlinger aboard, had a dice with Keke Rosberg for second place but this ended when Schumacher, exiting the pitlane after the first stop, found the rear of the C291 on fire and promptly pulled off.

The Jaguar's run was soon over, the starter motor's needing replacement at Warwick's pitstop and now a Peugeot one-two was on the cards. Sadly for them, the electrics on Yannick Dalmas' 905 packed up and left, ironically, Mauro Baldi to take victory in the sole remaining Peugeot, Jochen Mass bringing the C11 into second place and Manuel Reuter bringing the Kremer 962 in third. It appeared that there was still life in the old turbo cars yet, even though the C11 finished a lap down on the winner.

Once more, at Monza, the following month, it was a Jaguar XJR-14 on pole position, this time Teo Fabi's car. The C291 was out-qualified by Cor Euser's Spice SE90C, Schumacher being unable to match the English car's top speed on this very fast circuit.

Martin Brundle's Jaguar had to make an engine change after the morning warm-up and start from the pitlane in the race, but he was up to third place by the third lap and took second away from Rosberg's Peugeot by lap seven. Teo Fabi

Previous page: The Michael Schumacher/Karl Wendlinger-driven C291 at Autopolis, Mexico, where the pair won outright from Derek Warwick and David Brabham in a Jaguar XJR-14. [Photo: Courtesy of LAT.]

WORLD CHAMPIONS – THE GROUP C CARS

Mercedes mechanics swarm around the C291 of Jean-Louis Schlesser and Jochen Mass at the Nürburgring in 1991. Sadly, the gearbox failed after twenty-eight laps. They did, however, last longer than the second C291, that of Michael Schumacher and Karl Wendlinger, whose engine failed after just ten laps. [Photo courtesy of LAT.]

The opening lap of the 1991 Le Mans 24-Hours and the three Mercedes C11s are already leading. It was not to last. [Photo: Courtesy of LAT.]

had easily taken the lead from the start. Once again, Schlesser could not beat Manuel Reuter's Porsche 962C.

When Max Cohen-Olivar rolled his Salamin-entered Porsche 962C, a period of confusion arose, as the pace car could not find the leader. This was not surprising, as Teo Fabi had chosen this moment to pit! Another replacement starter motor had to be fitted to the XJR-14, dropping the Jaguar down to thirteenth place. The second Jaguar came back into the race in second place to the Yannick Dalmas-driven Peugeot, that car having got ahead in all the confusion. The C11 was, however, soon up to second place, albeit two laps behind.

Positions became stabilized after Dalmas entered his pit too fast and knocked over a mechanic (thankfully only slightly injuring him) and equipment. So much time was lost that, by the time that Keke Rosberg had driven out onto the track, the car was down in a lowly eighth place.

At the finish, the Jaguars were one and two, Derek Warwick having fairly easily overhauled the C11. The C291's engine had failed on lap twenty.

So to Silverstone on May 19th, where much work to slow this circuit for the Formula One cars had changed its character quite dramatically.

Once again the XJR-14 showed its superiority, the two Jaguars occupying the front row. Even the new Peugeots could not come within four seconds of them. The C291 was even slower. It certainly looked as though, for once, TWR-Jaguar had upped their game after being beaten for the last two seasons.

At the start, Teo Fabi drove off into the distance. Martin Brundle missed a gearshift and then had a throttle cable break, putting him well down but setting the scene for a great comeback drive.

Karl Wendlinger, in the C291, had a good dice with Keke Rosberg for second place. The Peugeot was demonstrably faster in a straight line, but Wendlinger closed in under braking, never really getting close enough to dive past. Rosberg's car then developed a misfire and dropped back, allowing the Sauber-Mercedes into a second place that it was not to lose.

Brundle charged back to third place, demoting the C11, which had finally got the better of Cor Euser's Spice for fourth, and finally the new C291 had a podium finish, although a lap down on the winning Jaguar.

This year, Le Mans was back as a part of the Championship. The 3.5-liter cars were obliged to run but neither Jaguar nor Mercedes were serious about running their "Atmo" cars. Both the C291 and the XJR-14 appeared for qualifying, the Jaguar posting a qualifying time on a par with Schlesser's C11 whilst the C291 did not run.

Three low-drag C11s were used to contest the Le Mans 24-Hour race in 1991. The wing was set lower and as far back as possible, necessitating the removal of the front splitter. The rear wing was, in fact, identical to that used on the C291. This wing allowed a change of flaps, which varied in size from 5 to 20 mm, in 3 mm increments. The sprint-type underbody was in place as well as the previously sealed over louvers above the front wheel arches.

Although both the Joest team, with their Porsche 962s, and TWR, with their Jaguar XJR-12's ran high-downforce bodywork, it was the Mercedes C11s that topped the time sheets in qualifying, Schlesser piloting his car around in 3:31.27 (almost 139 mph). These Le

Brake discs glowing orange hot in the night, one of the Mercedes C11s, that of Karl Wendlinger, Michael Schumacher and Fritz Kreuzpointer tries hard to stay in contention. Despite leading, this trio experienced gearbox problems and finished fifth, the highest placed Mercedes in 1991. Although on paper it should have been a Mercedes victory, niggling problems kept them from the winner's rostrum. [Photo: Courtesy of LAT.]

Lights ablaze, one of the Mercedes C11s heads into the night at Le Mans in 1991. [Photo: Courtesy of Daimler/Chrysler Archives.]

Mans C11s also differed from the usual 'sprint' version, in having a limited slip differential fitted, instead of the previously used spool. This modification reduced understeer in the cars. Tests had shown that the l.s.d.s would easily last for twenty-four hours of racing.

Obviously, for Mercedes, chief opposition appeared to be the TWR Jaguars, no fewer than six of which had been entered,

Around the second chicane on the Mulsanne straight comes the C11 of Wendlinger, Schumacher and Kreuzpointer. [Photo: Courtesy of LAT.]

four running with the engines enlarged to 7.4-liters. A dark horse entry was the Mazda team with three four-rotor 787s. The team was managed by six times Le Mans winner, Jackie Ickx. They only had to run at an 830 kg weight limit.

The first ten slots were reserved for the "Atmo" cars, even though the pole-

*Jean-Louis Schlesser.
[Photo: Courtesy of LAT.]*

sitting Peugeot 905 of Alliot/Jabouille/Baldi was some three seconds slower than the C11 of Schlesser/Mass and Ferte.

At the start, the Peugeots led but they were out by the time night fell, engine maladies disposing of them.

Mass now took the lead with Michael Schumacher in second place. Oscar Larrauri followed in a Joest-Porsche with Jonathan Palmer in the third C11 in fourth place. The best Jaguar was the Davy Jones/Raul Boesel/Michel Ferte car in fifth place.

Karl Wendlinger, Fritz Kreuzpointer and Michael Schumacher then took the lead in their C11 while the Palmer/Dickens C11 took over third place. While Kreuzpointer was in the C11, the Schlesser/Mass/A. Ferte C11 sister car overtook him. Wendlinger then nudged a wall and fell back to third place. The Porsches, despite showing early promise, fell back with a plethora of minor problems.

In the early hours of the morning, Palmer's car began to suffer with bad handling as the result of an earlier "off" and the Jones/Boesel/M. Ferte Jaguar was now up to third place.

At the twelve-hour mark, the Schumacher/Wendlinger/Kreuzpointer C11 was in the lead again, taking over from the Schlesser/Mass/Thiim C11. Both cars were three laps ahead of the third placed Jaguar. Fourth was now the Johnny Herbert/Volker Weidler/Bertrand Gachot-driven Mazda 787, which the trio had been driving flat out from the start.

During the morning, Wendlinger brought in the leading C11 with gearbox problems and the mechanics set to. By the time the car came out again, it had dropped to ninth place. Although the Schlesser/Mass/A. Ferte C11 had a very long lead, the drivers did not like the message that the temperature gauge was beginning to tell.

The Palmer/Dickens C11 then retired with a broken crankshaft damper caused by running over debris. More importantly, the Mazda had now pushed the Jaguar down into third place.

At one o'clock, the leading Mercedes pulled into the pits, its race run. An alternator bracket had broken, and, as this also supported the water pump, the engine had overheated. The Mazda screamed into a lead it would not now lose with three Jaguars following on.

At the finish, Johnny Herbert, the last driver in the Mazda, fainted in his father's arms as he climbed out of the winning car, so hard had the trio of young drivers had to drive to win. Probably not since the 1965 running, where the Masten Gregory/Jochen Rindt Ferrari 250 LM won, had a car driven so consistently fast, won the race. The best Mercedes could finish in this troubled year for them, was the fifth placed car of Michael Schumacher/Karl Wendlinger and Fritz Kreuzpointer.

Incidentally, they did manage to win the Index of Efficiency, one of Le Mans' curious side awards.

It was a long time until the next round of the SWC, this time taking place at the Nürburgring. It was here that a disturbing series of Mercedes engine failures began, when a batch of faulty blocks started to be used.

Martin Brundle had departed TWR for the Brabham F1 team, his place being filled by David Brabham. Mercedes brought in Harvey Postlethwaite to try and sort out the C291's problems. As had previously been the case with chassis building, Mercedes were not above asking the English for help on occasion, an indication that Motor racing was now a global sport. The Peugeot 905 now appeared with new bodywork, strikingly similar to that of the XJR-14, and the improvement was obvious, the new car being only slightly slower than the Jaguar.

Fabi's Jaguar took an immediate lead with, before long, the Peugeots running him close. Schumacher had the C291 up behind Baldi's Peugeot, and was in shortly to have his windshield cleaned of oil from the Peugeot. His drive back saw the engine let go: more a fault of a faulty engine block than the engine's design itself. He was not the only one to lose an engine. Not long after, Rosberg's Peugeot slid off into gravel as a result of a dropped valve. David Brabham then inherited the lead when Teo Fabi hit Jurgen Opperman whilst lapping the 962C, and spun.

By now, Baldi's Peugeot and Schlesser's C291 were involved in a dice for second place, but Schlesser was forced to retire when the gearbox started to fail. Baldi took this opportunity to pass David Brabham's Jaguar but that car was out shortly thereafter when the engine failed

This left the David Brabham/Derek Warwick car to win with the sister car, that of Teo Fabi and David Brabham, in second place. Derek Warwick now led the Drivers' Championship.

One month later, the circus gathered at Magny Cours, a circuit that should, and did, favor Peugeot. It was here that Michelin tested their tires, and had carried out many tests on the new Peugeot 905 Evo 1 Bis to make it more competitive. That they had succeeded was beyond doubt, as they not only finished one-two, but also took pole position (Dalmas) and fastest lap of the race (Alliot).

For Sauber-Mercedes, it was another bad race, Schumacher showing promise when he qualified third ahead of the Jaguars but then retiring when the coolant boiled dry after a hose clamp split, and Jochen Mass retiring the car that he was co-driving with Schlesser when the throttle return spring broke. The best that the XJR-14s could do was finish in third place, lapped twice by the winning French cars.

October 6th at Mexico City saw the penultimate race of the 1991 season.

As at so many races in this troubled season, the Sauber-Mercedes cars failed, despite Michael Schumacher setting the fastest lap of the race. At one point, Schumacher was up to second place before oil pump failure put him out and then Jochen Mass' car retired with electrical problems.

Keke Rosberg won again in the Peugeot, the team scoring another one-two, but the Peugeot revival was too late to stop TWR-Jaguar winning the SWC.

Sauber-Mercedes final race of 1991 (and, as it turned out, its final sports car race) took place on the Autopolis circuit of Japan. Teo Fabi took an XJR-14 and wrung its neck to take pole position, giving him a shot at the Drivers Championship that Derek Warwick looked like winning at this point. Toyota had brought along their new 3.5-liter contender, the TS010, and this placed fifth on the starting grid. The C291s could do no better than take the next two slots.

Yannick Dalmas led at the start, overwhelming Fabi when he missed a gearshift. Schumacher had taken third and Warwick stayed right behind him as these four tore off ahead of the rest of the pack. Schumacher then out-braked Fabi and, as he closed on the leader, Dalmas' engine let go and Schumacher now led the race. Fabi slipped back, concerned with preserving the XJR-11 to the end of the race, whilst staying ahead of Derek Warwick but in the end he had to let him by and settle for third place. Karl Wendlinger took over from Michael Schumacher and Derek Warwick tried hard to overtake the C291 but was continuously held up behind traffic.

And so, finally, the Sauber-Mercedes C291 won a race, the last it would ever run for, shortly afterwards, the team announced its retirement from sportscar racing. The World of F1 was beckoning.

Jochen Mass: "The C291 was terrific to drive. The handling was wonderful. The engine was like a turbine, the way it would rev to over 14,000 rpm. The problems that we faced were all with the peripherals. The advantage of using a 180 degree V-12 engine was lost with the gearbox raising it, plus all the engine management on top. It took far too long to change an engine."

"At Autopolis, Schumacher flew. We (Schlesser and Mass) couldn't keep up with him and Karl (Wendlinger)."

Jochen Mass retired from an illustrious racing career and lives today in Monte Carlo, still coaching drivers to be, if at all possible, as fast as he and, if that is not possible, to be at least fast, safe and competent.

Max Welti and Jochen Mass. [Photo: Courtesy of LAT.]

Jochen Mass stands between two of Mercedes' finest sports racing cars. On the left is the 300SLR which, driven by Stirling Moss (partnered by Dennis Jenkinson), won the 1955 Mille Miglia outright. On the right is the World Sportscar Championship-winning Sauber-Mercedes C9. [Photo: Courtesy of Daimler-Chrysler Archives.]

APPENDIX

Individual Cars' Histories

C5/01: BMW M1 engine

1981: Sold to Dieter Quester.
Le Mans 24-Hours: Quester/Surer/Deacon, DNF. (Engine.)

C5/02: BMW M1 engine

1981: Nürburgring 1000 Kms: Stuck/Piquet, 1st overall.

C6/01: Group C car: Cosworth DFL 3.9 engine

Sold to Walter Brun.

1982:
16/05: Silverstone 1000 Kms: Brun/Muller, 13th overall.
30/05: Nürburgring 1000 Kms: Stuck/Heyer, DNF. (Engine.)
05/09: Spa-Francorchamps 1000 Kms: Stuck/Heyer, 9th.
19/09: Mugello: Brun/Muller, 5th.
17/10: Brands Hatch 1000 Kms: Stuck, DNF.
Re-engined with BMW 1.7-liter turbo four-cylinder engine.

1983: Re-named "Sehcar"
Porsche-engined.
18-19/06: Le Mans 24-Hours: J. Villeneuve/L. Heimrath, Jr./D. Deacon, DNF.

1984:
23/04: Monza 1000 Kms: Rothengatter/C. Schickentanz, DNS.
13/05: Silverstone 1000 Kms: Rothengatter/Schickentanz, 15th.

Sold to Angelo Pallavicini.

2001: Sold on.

C6/02: Sold to GS Tuning.

Sold to Walter Brun. Cosworth 3.3-liter engine fitted.

Re-named: "Sehcar"

1983:
29/05: Nürburgring 1000 Kms: Brun, DNF. (Accident.) Car destroyed.

Another chassis/car built up by TC Prototypes.

18/06-19: Le Mans 24-Hours: Stuck/Grohs, DNS.

Sold to Roland Bassaler. M1 3.5-liter engine fitted.

1984:
15-16/06: Le Mans 24-Hours: R. Bassaler/D. Lacaud/I. Tapy, 23rd.

1986:
31/05-01/06: Le Mans 24-Hours: R. Bassaler/D. Lacaud/I. Tapy, #95, not classified.

1987:
13-14/06: Le Mans 24-Hours: Y. Hervalet/J-F. Yvon/H. Bourjade, #108, not classified.

1988:
11-12/06: Le Mans 24-Hours: R. Bassaler/J-F. Yvon/R. Pochauvin, #132, DNF. (Engine.)

2000: Sold to U.S.A. Vintage raced.

C7/01: BMW M1 engine

1983:
18-19/06:   Le Mans 24-Hours: T. Garcia/D. Montoya/A. Naon, 9th.
02/10:   Mt. Fuji 1000 Kms: F. Ballabio/M. Welti, 10th.
1984:
04/03:   Miami GP IMSA: Naon/W. Valiente/"Fomfor", 10th.
                Sold to "Fomfor".

1985:   366 cubic inch Chevrolet fitted.
11/08:   Mosport 1000 Kms: WEC: "Fomfor"/U. Bieri/M. Gysler, 7th.

C8/01:

1985:
17-18/06:   Le Mans 24-Hours: Nielsen/M. Welti/D. Quester, # 61, DNS.
                (Accident in practice.)

1986:
31/05-01/06:   Le Mans 24-Hours: H. Pescarolo/C. Danner/D. Quester, #62, DNF.
                (Gearbox.)

C8/02:

1986:
20/04:   Monza, Kouros Cup: J. Nielsen/H. Pescarolo, #61, 9th.
05/05:   Silverstone 1000 Kms: Thackwell/Nielsen/Pescarolo, 8th.
24/08:   Nürburgring 1000 Kms: Thackwell/Pescarolo, #61, 1st.
15/05:   Spa-Francorchamps 1000 Kms: Thackwell/Pescarolo, #61, 6th.

1987:
13-14/06: Le Mans 24-Hours: G. Lempereur/P-A Lombardi/J. Guillot, #42, DNF. (Gearbox.)
Sold to Noel del Bello.
26/07: Brands Hatch 1000 Kms: J-P. Jassaud/G. Lempereur/L. Rossiaud, #42, DNS. (Accident.)
30/08: Nürburgring 1000 Kms: J-P. Jassaud/G. Lempereur/L. Rossiaud, #42, DNF. (Gearbox.)
13/09: Spa-Francorchamps 1000 Kms: J-P. Jassaud/G. Lempereur/N. del Bello, #42, DNA.

1988:
10/04: Monza 1000 Kms: B. Santal/J. Guillot/R. Bianconne, #42, DNS. (Engine.)
11-12/06: Le Mans 24-Hours: B. Santal/N. del Bello/B. de Dryver, #42, DNF. (Engine.)
24/07: Brands Hatch 1000 Kms: H. Regout/B. Santal/Noel del Bello, #42, DNF. (Fuel pump.)
3-4/09: Nürburgring 1000 Kms: H. Regout/B. Santal/Noel del Bello, #42, DNA.
18/09: Spa-Francorchamps 1000 Kms: H. Regout/B. Santal/Noel del Bello, #42, DNA.

C8/03:

1986:
20/04: Monza: J. Nielsen/H. Pescarolo, #61, practice only, DNS.
05/05: Silverstone 1000 Kms: H. Pescarolo, #61, DNS. (Training car only.)
31/05-01/06: Le Mans 24-Hours: J. Nielsen/M. Thackwell/H. Pescarolo, #61, DNF. (Engine.)

SAUBER-MERCEDES

C9/01:

1987:
13-14/06:   Le Mans 24-Hours: M. Thackwell/H. Pescarolo/H. Okada, #32, DNF. (Gearbox.)
28/06:   Nuremberg 200 Miles: M. Thackwell/M. Reuter, #61, DNF. (Driver fatigue.)
30/08:   Nürburgring 1000 Kms: J. Dumfries/M. Thackwell/H. Pescarolo, #61, DNF. (Gearbox.)
13/09:   Spa-Francorchamps 1000 Kms: Thackwell/Schlesser, #62. (Training car only.)
            Re-chassised and re-numbered as C9/88-01.

C9/88-01:

1988:
06/03:   Jerez 300 Kms: Schlesser/Baldi/Mass, #61. (Training car only.)
13/03:   Jarama 360 Kms: Schlesser/Baldi, #61. (Training car only.)
24/04:   Monza 1000 Kms: Schlesser/Mass/Baldi, #61. (Training car only.)
08/05:   Silverstone 1000 Kms: J. L. Schlesser, #61. (Training car only.)
24/07:   Brands Hatch 1000 Kms: Mass, DNF. (Accident.)
20/11:   Sandown 360 Kms: Baldi/Johansson, #62, 2nd.
            In the Mercedes Museum, Stuttgart.

C9/02:

1987:
30/08:   Nürburgring 1000 Kms: J. Dumfries/M. Reuter, #62, DNS. (Accident.)
13/09:   Spa-Francorchamps 1000 Kms: Thackwell/Schlesser, #61, 7th. (Pole.)

1988:   (C9-88-02)
06/03:   Jerez 300 Kms: Schlesser/Baldi/Mass, #61, 1st.
13/03:   Jarama 360 Kms: Schlesser/Baldi, 2nd.

24/04:   Monza 1000 Kms: Schlesser/Mass/Baldi, 2nd.
11-12/06:   Le Mans 24-Hours: J. Mass/M. Baldi/J. Weaver, #61, DNS. (Tires.)
10/07:   Brno GP CSSR: Mass/Schlesser, #62, 1st.
24/07:   Brands Hatch 1000 Kms: Mass, #62, DNF. (Accident.)
10/09:   Fuji 1000 Kms: M. Baldi/P. Strieff, #62, NRF. (Accident.)

1989:
10-11/06:   Le Mans 24-Hours: Schlesser/Cudini/Jabouille, #62, 5th.
25/06:   Jarama: Baldi/Acheson, #61, 5th.
23/07:   Brands Hatch: Baldi/Acheson, #61, 1st.
23/08:   Nürburgring: Baldi/Acheson, #61, 2nd.
03/09:   Possibly, Donington: J-L. Schlesser, #62. (Training car only.)
29/10:   Possibly, Mexico City: M. Baldi/J-L. Schlesser, #62. (Training car only.)
              In the Mercedes Museum, Stuttgart.

C9-88-03:

1988:
08/05:   Silverstone 1000 Kms: Schlesser/Mass, 2nd.
11-12/06:   Le Mans 24-Hours: J. Mass/K. Acheson/K. Niedwitz, #62, DNS. (Tires.)
10/07:   Brno CCS: M. Baldi/J. Weaver, #61, 4th.
24/07:   Brands Hatch 1000 Kms: Baldi/Schlesser, #61, 3rd.
3-4/09:   Nürburgring 1000 Kms: Schlesser/Mass, #61, 1st.
18/09:   Spa-Francorchamps 1000 Kms: Mass/Schlesser, #61, 3rd.
09/10:   Mount Fuji 1000 Kms: Mass/Acheson/Schlesser, 5th.
20/11:   Sandown 360 Kms: Schlesser/Mass, #61, 1st.

1989:
09/04:   Suzuka 480 Kms: K. Acheson, #62, 2nd.
21/05:   Dijon-Prenois: J-P. Schlesser/J. Mass, #62, 2nd.
10-11/06:   Le Mans 24-Hours: Mass/Reuter/Dickens, #63, 1st.
              In the Mercedes Museum, Stuttgart.

C9-88-04:

1988:
3-4/09:   Nürburgring 1000 Kms: Baldi/Johansson, DNF. (7th in first heat, two accidents in second heat.)
18/09:   Spa-Francorchamps 1000 Kms: Baldi/Johansson, #62, 1st.
09/10:   Mount Fuji 1000 Kms: Baldi/Streiff, DNF. (Accident.)
20/11:   Sandown 360 Kms:

1989:
09/04:   Suzuka 480 Kms: Schlesser/Baldi, #61, 1st.
21/05:   Dijon-Prenois: Baldi/Acheson, #61, 3rd.
10-11/06:   Le Mans 24-Hours: Baldi/Acheson/Brancatelli, #61, 2nd.
23/07:   Brands Hatch: Schlesser/Mass, #62, 3rd.
                      In the Mercedes Museum, Stuttgart.

C9-88-05:

1989:   # 62
21/05:   Dijon: J-L. Schlesser/J-P. Jabouille, #61. (Training car only.)
10-11/06:   Le Mans 24-Hours: J-P. Jabouille/J-P. Schlesser/A. Cudini, #62. (Training car only.)
23/07:   Brands Hatch: Schlesser/Mass, #61. (Training car only.)
23/08:   Nürburgring: Schlesser/Mass, #62, 1st.
03/09:   Donington: Schlesser/Mass, #62, 1st.
17/09:   Spa-Francorchamps: Schlesser/Mass: #62, NRF.
29/10:   Mexico City: Schlesser/Mass, #62, 1st.

1990:
08/04:   Suzuka: Schlesser/Baldi, #1, 1st.

                      Sold to a customer in Europe.

C9-88-06:

1989:	# 61
03/09:	Donington: Baldi/Acheson, #61, 2nd.
17/09:	Spa-Francorchamps: Baldi/Acheson, #61, 1st.
29/10:	Mexico City: M. Baldi/K. Acheson, #61, DNF. (Accident.)
1990:	
08/04:	Suzuka: Mass/Wendlinger, #2, 2nd.
29/04:	Monza: Spare car.
	In the Mercedes Museum, Stuttgart.

C11-01:

1990:	
08/04:	Suzuka: Schlesser, #1, DNQ. (Spare car.)
29/04:	Monza: Mass/Wendlinger, #2, 2nd.
20/05:	Silverstone: Mass/Schumacher, #2, DNS. (Disqualified.)
03/06:	Spa-Francorchamps: Mass/Wendlinger, #2, 1st.
22/07:	Dijon-Prenois: Mass/Schumacher, #2. (Training car only.)
19/08:	Nürburgring: Mass/Schumacher, #2, 2nd.
02/09:	Donington: J. Mass/H-H. Frentzen, #2, 2nd.
23/09:	Montreal: Schlesser/Baldi: #1. (Training car only.)
07/10:	Mexico City: J-P. Schlesser/M. Baldi/Schumacher, #2. (Training car only.)

C11-02:

1990:	
29/04:	Monza: Schlesser/Baldi, #1, 1st.
20/05:	Silverstone: Schlesser/Baldi, #1, DNF. (Engine.)
03/06:	Spa-Francorchamps: Baldi/Schlesser, #1, 8th.

Sauber-Mercedes

22/07:	Dijon-Prenois: Mass/Schumacher, #2, 2nd.
19/08:	Nürburgring: Mass/Schumacher, #2. (Training car only.)
07/10:	Mexico City: Mass/Schumacher, #2, 1st.

C11-03:

1990:
20/05:	Silverstone: Schlesser/Baldi, #1. (Training car only.)
03/06:	Spa-Francorchamps: Baldi/Schlesser, #1.(Training car only.)
22/07:	Dijon-Prenois: Schlesser/Baldi, #1, 1st.
19/08:	Nürburgring: Schlesser/Baldi, #1, 1st.
02/09:	Donington: Schlesser/Baldi #1, 1st.
23/09:	Montreal: Schlesser/Baldi: #1, 1st.

C11-04:

1990:
02/09:	Donington: Mass/Frentzen. (Training car only.)
23/09:	Montreal: Mass/Wendlinger, #2, 9th.

C11-05:

Michael Lauer, in C11-05, lapping a Porsche 956 at Daytona during an HSR race. [Photo: Courtesy of Daniel Mainzer.]

1990:
07/10:   Mexico City: Schlesser/Baldi, #1. Disqualified. (Actually 1st.)

1991:
14/04:   Suzuka: J-L. Schlesser/J. Mass, #1, 2nd.
05/05:   Monza: J-L. Schlesser/J. Mass, #1, 3rd.
19/05:   Silverstone: J-L. Schlesser/J. Mass, #1, 4th.
22-23/06:   Le Mans 24-Hours: K. Wendlinger/M. Schumacher/F. Kreuzpointer, #31, 5th.

2001:   Sold to Michael Lauer, U.S.A.

C291-01:   Retained by Sauber/Mercedes as test and development car.
               In the Mercedes Museum, Stuttgart.

C291-02:

1991:
14/04:   Suzuka: K. Wendlinger/M. Schumacher, #2, DNF. (Fire.)
05/05:   Monza: K. Wendlinger/M. Schumacher, #2, DNF. (Engine.)
19/05:   Silverstone: K. Wendlinger/M. Schumacher, #2, 2nd.
18/08:   Nürburgring: M. Schumacher/K. Wendlinger, #2, DNS. (Training car only.)
15/09:   Magny Cours: M. Schumacher/K. Wendlinger, #2, DNS. (Training car only.)
06/10:   Mexico City: J-L. Schlesser/J. Mass, #1, DNS. (Training car only.)
27/10:   Autopolis: J-L. Schlesser/J. Mass, #1, DNS. (Training car only.)
               In the Mercedes Museum, Stuttgart.

C291-03:

1991:
18/10:   Nürburgring: M. Schumacher/K. Wendlinger, #2, DNF. (Engine.)
15/09:   Magny Cours: M. Schumacher/K. Wendlinger, #2, DNF. (Leaking coolant.)
27/10:   Autopolis: J-L. Schlesser/J. Mass, #1, 5th.
                In the Mercedes Museum, Stuttgart.

C291-04:

1991:
06/10:   Mexico City: M. Schumacher/K. Wendlinger, #2, DNF. (Oil pump.)
27/10:   Autopolis: M. Schumacher/K. Wendlinger, #2, 1st.
                In the Mercedes Museum, Stuttgart.

C291-05:

1991:
18/08:   Nürburgring: J-L. Schlesser/J. Mass, #1, DNF. (Gearbox.)
15/09:   Magny Cours: J-L. Schlesser/J. Mass, #1, DNF. (Throttle cable.)
06/10:   Mexico City: J-L. Schlesser/J. Mass, #1, NRF. (Electrical.)
                In the Mercedes Museum, Stuttgart.

C293-01:   Never raced. At the Sauber factory.

C293-02:   Never raced. At the Sauber factory.

Focus on these other great titles ...

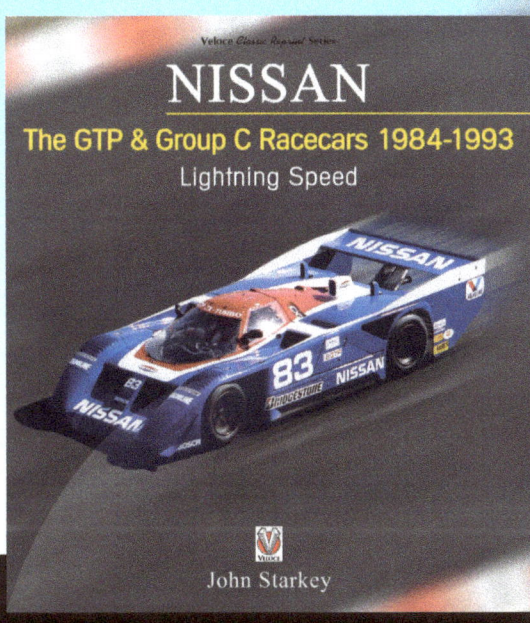

Detailing the development and racing achievements of the Nissan GTP and Group C Racecars. Contains revealing interviews with some of the drivers and designers involved, and an appendix detailing the history of each car.

- V5404 • Hardback • 22.8x20.8cm
- 160 pages • 115 pictures
- ISBN: 978-1-787114-94-4
- UPC: 6-36847-01494-0

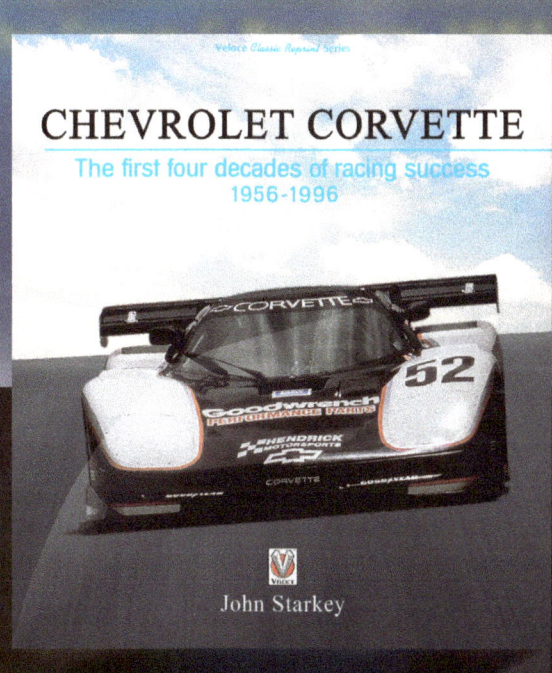

This book takes a detailed look at the racing Chevrolet Corvette from its inception, construction, and its subsequent updates through the years.

- V5405 • Hardback • 22.8x20.8cm
- 192 pages • 162 pictures
- ISBN: 978-1-787114-92-0
- UPC: 6-36847-01492-6

www.veloce.co.uk
www.velocebooks.com

The hard SL ...

Like a bit of Mercedes? You could do a lot worse than check out Brian Long's extensively – even exhaustively – researched Mercedes-Benz series.

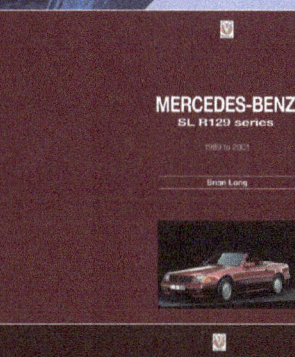

Above from left to right: Veloce's comprehensive SL & SLK range of books from Brian Long: includes SL 113 1963 to 1971, SL/SLC 107 series, SL R129 1989 to 2001, SL R230 2001 to 2011 and SLK titles R170 1996 to 2004, and also includes R171 2004-2011.

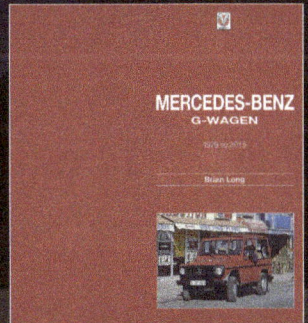

Also available:
The G-Wagen – Mercedes' viable answer to the Land Rover has a cult status and an off-road ability to shame a mountain goat – the story is all here in painstaking detail.

The pillarless design of the Mercedes W123 coupé turned heads in the latter part of the last century and are very collectible today.

www.veloce.co.uk
www.velocebooks.com

PORSCHE 930 to 935
The Turbo Porsches

In 1974, to rave reviews, Porsche produced the 930/911 Turbo to the public and set off on a new road. At the same time, the governing body of motorsport introduced a new "silhouette" formula to sports car racing. Thus the immortal 934 and 935 were born.
This book tells the story of the 911 Turbo and its racing cousins, from the 1974 2.1-litre RSR Turbo Carrera to the tube-framed 750 horsepower final variants of the 935. These are the cars which still bring a gleam of pleasure to any of the drivers lucky enough to have sampled their enormous power and, sometimes, their wayward handling!

V5246 • Hardback • 23.114x20.828cm • 304 pages • 252 pictures
• ISBN: 978-1-787112-46-9 • UPC: 6-36847-01246-5

www.ingramcontent.com/pod-product-compliance
Lightning Source LLC
Chambersburg PA
CBHW041411300426
44114CB00028B/2984